BECOMING THE MOTHER OF

 *Me*

My mother and I, a child of four years, I believe, in front of the home of friends in Minneapolis. These friends were caring for us while my father was in the hospital for some unremembered reason. Unremembered, too, is the doll! Where did she come from? Where did she go? Was mothering already a problem at four years of age?

BECOMING THE MOTHER OF

Me

A Memoir

Kathryn Adams Doty

EDINBOROUGH PRESS

2008

Edinborough Press
  P. O. Box 13790
  Roseville, Minnesota 55117
  1-888-251-6336
  www.edinborough.com
  books@edinborough.com

The text is composed in Garamond Premier Pro and printed on acid-free paper.

LIBRARY OF CONGRESS CATALOGING-IN-PUBLICATION DATA
  Doty, Kathryn Adams, 1920-
  Becoming the mother of me : a memoir / Kathryn Adams Doty.
    p. cm.
  ISBN 978-1-889020-27-3 (alk. paper)
    1. Doty, Kathryn Adams, 1920- 2. Authors, American—20th century—
Biography. 3. Motion picture actors and actresses—United States—Biography. 4.
Child psychologists—United States—Biography. I. Title.
  PS3604.O89Z46 2008
  813'.54—dc22

          2007041914

Contents

Dedication vii

Years of Then 1

Chapter One 3

Chapter Two 9

Chapter Three 17

Chapter Four 23

Chapter Five 29

Chapter Six 35

Chapter Seven 40

Chapter Eight 45

Chapter Nine 50

Chapter Ten 56

Chapter Eleven 61

Chapter Twelve 66

Chapter Thirteen 71

Chapter Fourteen 76

Chapter Sixteen 88

Chapter Seventeen 93

Chapter Eighteen 98

Chapter Nineteen 102

Chapter Twenty 109

Chapter Twenty-one 115

Chapter Twenty-two 119

Chapter Twenty-three 128

Days of Now 134

My family, 1923
Back row: Hero brother Roland, "Nichsnutz" Winfried
Front row: Mama, Me, Father

"Nichtsnutz" in German means "good-for-nothing" but in our family it took on the more tolerant tone of "mischief-maker."

∽ Dedication ∽

"I thank all who have loved me in their hearts, with love and thanks from mine." Elizabeth Barrett Browning wrote these words long ago; and yet, in this moment now, they express all that I feel as I look back at the process of writing the story of my life.

Most importantly, writing my my memoir was my way of paying tribute and expressing gratitude to my unusually fine parents, Christian Gottlieb Hohn, Anna Marie Rockel Hohn, and also to my brothers, Roland G. Hohn and Winfried Christian Hohn. It is to these members of my family of origin that I dedicate my memoir, *Becoming the Mother of Me*.

Other names come to mind, of greatly loved friends whose listening ears and nonjudgmental hearts re-lived with me those persons, events, joys and sorrows, conflicts and struggles of my life's journey. As we shared our memories, we became "story-tellers" in the tradition of many cultures of the world, keeping alive persons and happenings that otherwise may very well have been forgotten. In the last few years, eight of these dearest of friends have passed away, and I regret not letting them know more fully how much I treasured their friendship. It is never too late to breathe "Thank You" as I remember them.

Then, there are those who carefully read my manuscript, offering detailed and valuable reactions and suggestions. Thank you, Jane Shostag, poet Sue Chambers, Diann Marten, Rich and Nancy Helgeson, and Suzanne Bunkers.

I acknowledge and honor my indebtedness to Hugh Beaumont, my first husband and father of our three most wonderful children, Hunter, Kristan and Mark. It was Hugh who illuminated parts of life from which my childhood and adolescent years had shielded me. I honor his intelligence, his talent, his worldly wisdom. I wanted to share some of the stories of our life together, but because he is no longer living to tell his own tale, I also tried to respect and honor his desire and need for the sacredness of privacy.

I acknowledge the great gift of the love and caretaking of Fred Doty, whose life has been deeply entwined with mine as husband and wife for almost thirty years. During my writing we shared tears and laughter as he listened daily to my story as it unfolded, commented wisely, fed me (and our two cats), ran errands — and corrected my spelling!

Love and thanks to all of you!

Kathryn Adams Doty

BECOMING THE MOTHER OF

 *Me*

∽ *Years of Then* ∽

"I am a camera with its shutter open, quite passive, recording, not thinking.
Recording the man shaving at the window opposite and the woman in
the kimono washing her hair. Someday this will all have to be developed,
carefully printed, fixed." — Christopher Isherwood, *Goodbye to Berlin*

I cannot sing the words that tell my life
so dulling down the endless deep of less

Eight score years and six.
I stand before the door of dark tomorrow
one hand against the wall to brace me straight.
I use the other one to flick the switch.
No light illuminates the emptiness before me
the fade-out of my graying days.

Had I been a camera in all the years behind me
I might well have made and fixed
a record of it all.

In my younger years, close-ups only
one face alone, until each wrinkle of my soul
revealed me.

Now, in age, I open the shutters of my mind.
I pull the dolly back
for the long shot of my life.
I change the lens of my understanding,
sharpen the focus.

A multitude appears before me.
He and she and they laugh aloud, and weep
bend in failure, rise in joy.

Their dance of life intertwines with mine
and the distant past comes alive once more.
In memory, I walk into that past and dance with them
lively as my crumbling bones allow.
Lights! Camera! Action! Sound!

Chapter One

The first voice I hear is my mother's, the Mama of my earliest years: "You know," she begins, as she crochets her way through the story of my birth, "my first and only daughter, Kathryn Elizabeth Hohn, was born July 15, 1920, in New Ulm, Minnesota's Loretto Hospital.

"Her father, Christian Hohn, was minister of the Methodist Church in New Ulm, and when I was in labor he walked every step of the way up and down the corridors of the hospital with me, then had to kiss me goodbye when I went into the delivery room. Husbands weren't allowed in, then. But I wasn't scared. I was fully conscious when she was born. Didn't want the ether because it made me hemorrhage, so I remember everything. And when she finally came out, Dr. Strickler caught her in his big hands, lifted her way up in the air so I could see her and said, 'Anna Marie, it's a baby girl.' And I fainted dead away!"

This — my grand entrance onto the stage of this world.

As the years went by, I was filled in on more details of my birth from my mother. She had two sons eight and thirteen years older than I, and she and my father longed for a girl to complete their family. Before she became pregnant with me, she had had three full-term still births, one of which was a girl. Cesarean sections were uncommon then, so these three still births were near death experiences for my mother. And yet she never thought of giving up trying to have a daughter and she never once complained or filled me with apprehension about childbirth.

She very matter-of-factly told me that the doctors had said she had an infantile uterus, whatever that meant. But that didn't mean she couldn't give birth normally, they said.

"You don't have an infantile uterus, I bet," she would say. "You have the Hohn hips. You are built to have children."

Many years later, in my teenage excitement about becoming a psychiatrist someday — I had just read Alexis Carrel's *Man, the Unknown* — my father wrote this letter to me and left it on the night table by my bed.

> My dear daughter,
>
> If I may be permitted I would like to share with you a little secret which is in the heart of your mother's and mine, and which, I think, will illustrate

the promising anticipations I have of the kind of work in which you seem so deeply interested.

When your mother and I were expressing the desire to each other that the Good Lord would favor us with a daughter of our own, long before you were born, or even on the way, both of us knelt down and prayed that the child with which He may bless us might be possessed of the Christ spirit and nature and become thoroughly devoted to Him and His Kingdom. We were both desperately in earnest about it and with these hopes in our hearts we looked forward to your coming.

We have watched your development with keen interest, so far, and I have a conviction that the tendencies of your nature have been largely conditioned by our own desires, even in your prenatal development.

Blessings on you, my dear child. In my thoughts I can see your Guardian Angel accompanying you in all your ways. There is no doubt in my mind that the good Lord of Life will make you a blessing for Mankind.

Your affectionate Father

And so, you see, I came in to this world with a heavy-laden destiny, one which neither my father nor my mother ever meant to be a burden, only a testimony that I was very much longed for and greatly loved. I was born to fulfill my parent's deepest longing, the answer to their heartfelt prayers. I was born to be the perfect "preacher's daughter."

For the first eighteen years of my life, I tried with all my strength to fulfill their dream. I have a written evidence of this effort on my part. In this, my eighty-sixth year, I have read the entries in my very first journal. With embarrassment, but also tenderness for the twelve-year old who wrote it, I share with you now the dedication, the first page of this little diary printed in my unruly left handed printing:

I
Kathryn Elizabeth Hohn
do dedicate this book of Thoughts and Ideals to
to the perfection of my character

What follows are pages and pages of heartfelt pleas to the Almighty and to Jesus Christ, his Son, for help in becoming a shadowless, perfect person!

(That perfect, shadowless person was called, for the first eighteen years of her life, the short, sweet name "Betty" after my middle name Elizabeth. My mother often called me Katya, influenced by her German-from-Russia heritage, but she was the only one to use that nickname, much preferred by me. My father didn't want me nicknamed "Kate" after Kathryn, because they had a mule named "Kate." So down into the depths of my unruly psyche, mulishness, anger, and the demands of deepening sexuality, as well as the desire to be the "one and only," were pushed down into my unconscious, hidden from the world — but not forgotten!)

And then in February 1939, one telephone call changed my life forever.

Even now, sixty-six years later, back in touch with the long view of my life, I remember all this as though it happened yesterday. What happened, what I was thinking and feeling so long ago, floods my mind. It is as though I stepped into the film and was now a part of it, not just an observer.

The call came during my sophomore year as a student at Hamline University in St. Paul, Minnesota. I was singing in our college choir in St. Louis Park, our last Twin Cities concert before going on tour. I was the lead alto in the second alto section, hypnotized by our director, Mr. Jan Kuypers, enthralled with Bach, and heady with the feeling of group togetherness and accomplishment that singing in a fine choir provides. It was during the intermission of the concert that the call came. It came from the local RKO distributor, through to my mother, who was house mother in the annex to the college dormitory where we both lived, through to the Dean of Women, who knew where Hamline choir members were, through to the office of the St. Louis Park Methodist Church.

I was called to the phone by a stunned church secretary.

"Miss Hahn? Miss Kathryn Hahn?" Always that mispronunciation! I was put off right away.

"Hohn. Yes. Kathryn Hohn, long o!"

"Well, Kathryn, congratulations. You have just won the Gateway to Hollywood contest for the entire Midwest! Amazing good fortune. You are to leave for Hollywood tomorrow!"

Silence.

"Miss Hohn? Kathryn?"

Finally, my whispered, "Yes?"

"Did you hear me, Kathryn? Did we get disconnected?"

"No — I mean — yes. I think I heard you."

"Well, what do you say?"

"Well, I — I don't know — I — "

"You don't know! My God, Kathryn, do you know what this means? This is a lifetime opportunity! You've been chosen out of all the girls in the Midwest, north to south! To go to Hollywood, and appear on the radio — with a Hollywood star!"

Silence.

"What's the matter with you, Miss Hahn? Excuse me — Hohn? Are you okay?"

"I — I don't know. I think I'm OK. But, you see, I'm singing in the choir. We're going on tour tomorrow. I — I — "

"My God, Kathryn!"

How could this unseen man possibly understand the panic pouring through my body, running down my legs, opening the ground beneath my feet? What could he know about the sense of betrayal I was feeling, sending shock waves through me? The very best year and a half of my eighteen years of life gleamed before me and I had to face leaving it all — tomorrow! This man couldn't know I would be abandoning my widowed mother — tomorrow. I would be leaving my dearest of friends, my beloved choir director and fellow choir members, sopranos, altos, tenors, basses, Bach himself, my own dreams and ambitions of some day becoming a doctor, or college professor, or writing a great novel, fulfilling my beloved father's dreams for me, none of which included going to HOLLYWOOD! And I had to make the decision *now*, in a moment, on the telephone? How could I talk, much less think!

"Kathryn — are you there?"

"Yes — I — I suppose so."

"Kathryn," his voice softer now. Did he sense the bewilderment in my voice and in my silences? "Didn't you think when you entered the contest that you just might win?"

"Well, no, I — Miss Simley, our speech and drama coach, you see, just thought two of us, a boy and a girl, should enter the contest to see what it was like. The Hollywood scout sent to try us out on the radio couldn't get anyone promising in the Twin Cities to enter the contest. This being Minnesota, you see. We're sort of — well — you know — (I couldn't think of what we were that made us so wary of Hollywood. Had Minnesota Nice been invented?) So he called the college drama departments in and around the Twin Cities and got Miss Simley. That's how it happened. I didn't think about winning!"

"This is a rare opportunity, you know, Kathryn," the reasoning voice went on. "The winner of the contest will have a six-month contract with RKO. If things don't work out for you, you can come back. You'll only be gone three weeks if you don't win the national contest. Anyway, your round-trip train ticket is already bought. You'll have a roomette, and when you get there you will get room and board at the Studio Club and twenty-five dollars a week."

Thoughts, real practical thoughts, started to break through my panic. Twenty-five dollars a week for three weeks! That was a lot of money. Enough to pay my tuition at Hamline for one whole semester.

Ever since my father's death, my mother and I had been skimping along on only two meager minister's pensions, a bit for me until I was eighteen, a bit more for her for life. The president of the college, Dr. Charles Nelson Pace, had offered my mother the job of house-mothering in an annex to the girl's dormitory, helping to fulfill a promise to my father that he would see to it that I got a college education.

That was helpful, but we needed extra cash for clothes, food, books; and now that I was eighteen, no longer getting my eighteen dollars a month preacher's kid pension, there was nothing left over of the widow's mite for any of these things. So now! Here came an opportunity to earn enough for next semester's tuition. Solace started to creep into my fuzzy brain.

The unknown man was going on. "And think, Kathryn, of the opportunity. And what you'll do for Hamline University and the Twin Cities of Minnesota!"

There. That did it. Now there was a purpose, a thinking-of-others meaning to this shocking proposal. Little did he realize he had touched the minister's-daughter button: God first, others second, me last! The panic inside me was slowly fading and I managed a weak response. "Oh. Well. Of course. I'll just have to tell Mr. Kuypers. I'll have to go home and wash my hair."

"Kathryn Hohn, congratulations!" Relief in the man's voice. "And good luck. We'll be pulling for you! Your ticket will be delivered to your house tonight. Are you okay now?"

"Yes, I'm fine. Thank you."

And we both hung up.

But I wasn't fine. After the shock — tears. Tears were surging up inside me. They filled my eyes, blinding me. Intermission was over. Time to walk back on stage. To sing! How could I? Tomorrow I would be leaving this much-loved choir. How could they get along without me? (As though I was the only alto voice in the whole world!)

How could I tell Mr. Kuypers? Through my tears I saw that he already knew. Fellow altos, sopranos, tenors, basses had gathered around the phone as I talked and passed on the news. Tall, dignified, straight-backed, Mr. Kuypers sent a brief, warm smile my way.

"Congratulations, Kathryn. That is wonderful. Go to Hollywood. Have an adventure. Learn all you can and come back. Your place will be waiting for you."

That was all I needed. Following the sopranos, I filed back onto the stage as erect as I could, in my black robe with the red velvet trim, and sang, through my tears, "Lord Hosannah to the Son of David!" To keep my heart from breaking, I sang.

"Lord Hosannah! Lord Hosannah!"

I never went back. I have wondered often, all through the years, if the waiting place had been filled by me, what my life would have been like. That, I will never know.

Chapter Two

O N THE BUS RIDE BACK TO THE HAMLINE CAMPUS and the Annex that was home, I was too benumbed to think. I can't remember if my fellow choir members talked to me or not. All I remember was a swirl of feelings, a tiny ping of excitement; but mostly fear, fear of the Great Unknown mixed with a heavy sadness. I wondered for a moment what my mother would think about all this, the first time we would have been parted for any length of time since my father's death two years before. I took for granted that she would survive. But my father, my wonderful father, who held such high and mighty hopes for me, if he were living, what would he think?

I pushed away the fear that crept back into my being and walked in the door. The first thing I heard was my roommates clumping down the stairs. They clustered around me, excited as puppies. They hugged me and chattered away, offering information (one of the girls had even been to Southern California once!), asking if I wanted to borrow any clothes, dresses, scarves, jewelry. My meager wardrobe was too dark and heavy for California.

"Don't forget us," they said. "Don't 'Go Hollywood!' Come back!"

I knew very well what "Going Hollywood" meant. It meant abandoning all the solid values one had learned from babyhood. It meant becoming unreal and glamorized and so in love with oneself, nothing but fame and fortune mattered at all. No chance, I thought. Not me! Ever!

My mother did not appear. I thought I would find her in the kitchen, maybe preparing a healthy sack lunch for me to eat on my long train journey. As soon as I disentangled myself from the girls and walked into the kitchen, I saw her, not cooking, but washing my stockings and underwear and dusting our one, somewhat battered, suitcase. She was bustling with the brisk efficiency I have always envied, a gift that my daughter, not I, inherited.

Mama hugged me and, smiling through tears, said, "Why, Kathy, can you believe this! What would your father think? Would he let you go? Are we doing the right thing? Going off all that long way to — to Hollywood! All by yourself?"

"I don't know, Mama, but it's too late now. My ticket is coming tonight and I'm supposed to leave tomorrow! You know I can come back. Trains go both ways, you know."

Without another protest, my warm, round, sturdy mother hugged me, han-kied tears away, and got busy helping me pack while I washed my hair. My ticket was delivered soon, by a special messenger, my first taste of extraordinary privilege!

I don't think anyone in the Annex slept much that night. But I believe there must have been six or seven alarm clocks set, wound, ready to ring at five A.M. We were supposed to be at the depot at the crack of dawn. My considerate boyfriend drove my mother and me to the Great Northern station.

On the way we passed the exalted thirty-story, 792-foot Foshay Tower, where the fateful radio audition at WCCO on the top floor had been held such a short time ago. I waved goodbye to that imposing skyscraper and pulled the fake fur collar of my winter coat close around me. It was forty degrees below zero and a heavy snow had fallen recently. It didn't occur to me to be glad I was getting out of this ice-box weather. I had lived with it just fine for eighteen years.

We found the section of the train that held the roomettes (something I hadn't known even existed). There, waiting for me, were publicity men with cameras, the RKO representative, and a whole troupe of fellow students from the Hamline Drama Club. One of the members held a huge bouquet of red roses in his arms, and just before the conductor shouted "Board!" he thrust them at me.

There was only time for brief hugs, "good luck–goodbye–come back." I fumbled awkwardly with my suitcase, still clutching the roses. The porter took my suitcase and the flowers, helped me up the steps, showed me to my empty roomette, put the flowers back into my arms and, with a warm smile on his face, left me alone.

I looked out the window at my classmates, smiling, waving almost frantically, and I frantically smiled and waved back. In front of the troupe stood my mother with a very special boyfriend standing protectively close to her. I saw her trying to smile, too, waving her fingers just a little. Through the glass window that separated us, I watched her press her white handkerchief to her mouth to stifle the tears I just knew must be filling her eyes. In my bleary brain, I could just hear her say, "Please, my dear daughter, don't go!"

The train slowly pulled out, the waving figures growing smaller until they were out of sight, and it was then the dammed-up fear and confusion broke free. With two dozen roses still clutched in my arms, I burst into tears that seemed to have no end.

This was my send-off from the Twin Cities of Minnesota to Hollywood, California, February 1939.

February 1939
"Goodbye, goodbye to everything. . . . Leaving the known of snow and spring, of books and friends and learning to sing."

Until that moment of departure, the conflicts and anxieties I felt about leaving for Hollywood so suddenly and unexpectedly, had not included my mother's reaction and welfare. It never occurred to me to ask her permission, even though I was only eighteen.

Ever since my father's death and up until that very moment when the call from Hollywood came, I felt I was in charge of my life, at last. I never doubted that my mother's desire was to help fulfill my father's longings for me. It didn't occur to me that she had fantasies of her own about my life and her role in it. All the gathering of pieces of sterling silver and all the stitching of sheets and pillow cases for my hope chest sent no deep messages to me. It didn't enter my mind that there may have been some conflict between my mother and my father regarding my destiny, if he had lived. His words alone, had become my soul's desire. "Finish your education, my dear daughter. Become a fine Christian woman, a beacon and a service to mankind."

With two dozen roses in my arms, my coat and hat still on, and no knowledge of how roomettes worked, I hadn't shut the door. I didn't know there was one. So it was only a short while before the friendly porter stopped by and asked if I wanted him to take the roses and put them in a vase of water and perhaps lift my suitcase into the space above and maybe hang my coat for me.

His kindness was such a relief from my fear and sorrow, I gratefully let myself be waited on. He left with the roses, came back with all of them in one beautiful vase, pulled down the little table under the window and set them before me, leaving the door open.

It wasn't long before there was a soft knock. I turned my head and saw a very attractive young woman smiling at me. "Excuse me? I don't mean to intrude, but I saw the cameras and the crowd around you and I couldn't help wondering what was happening. I'm a journalist on my way to Palm Springs for a convention. Is there a chance you would like to have dinner with me?"

I must say, I brightened at the idea and agreed to meet her in the dining car around six, a long day away. But I had brought a textbook or two along with me to study so that I wouldn't be too far behind when I came back to school and I nibbled the healthy sack lunch my mother had made for me, the last snack lunch I would enjoy for a long, long time.

I settled down as best I could and started to read the assigned chapters.

It wasn't long before there was another knock, soon another and another, inviting me to breakfast, lunch, dinner for the next days of our long trip across the continent.

During dinner, I noticed other passengers nodding at me, smiling. My new journalist friend gently asked me what was sending me to far off Southern California, and I told her my story. She filled me in a little about what I might expect in Hollywood, and then, stirring her coffee, leaned across the table, smiled, and whispered, as though she were about to tell me a secret:

"Do you know, Kathryn, what the other passengers in this car thought when they saw the newsmen and cameras, the crowd, the three dozen roses, the girl who climbed aboard alone and was found by the porter, crying? We all assumed you were a bride who had been stood up by the groom!"

That was the first laugh I'd had in hours and hours and I must say, the friendly, curious passengers treated me all during the trip as though I were already a celebrity. I tasted my first oysters on the half shell, carefully sipped my first wine, remembering Mr. Kuypers saying, "Go to Hollywood. Have an adventure!" And for the first time in all these hours since the summons came, I began to think, just maybe, it would be possible!

However, as the morning came for the end of the trip, my anxiety crept back and prickled my skull. Someone was supposed to meet me. But how would I recognize him, or he me? If he didn't show up, where was I supposed to go? How would I get there?

The train whooshed to a steamy stop. My friendly fellow passengers said, "Goodbye. Good luck!" The porter handed me my suitcase and helped me down the stairs. I don't remember what I did with the roses.

Palm trees and sunshine emerged from engine steam. And that's when I saw him, the man who was to meet me. How did I know? Unmistakably Hollywood. A rather short dapper man with a small, trim mustache, smoking a cigarette in a cigarette holder and sporting a boutonniere in his lapel! He seemed to recognize me, too! Unmistakably Minnesota? Train weary, with flat-heeled shoes? How could he miss me?

He held out his hand, picked up my suitcase, took my elbow and started escorting me to the waiting limousine.

That's when I saw the other greeters, standing quietly to one side: a rather confident, amply framed woman wearing a hat with a fringe of flowers on the brim; beside her, a shorter, rather thin man with his head ducked down a bit, as though he were apologizing for being. But he did have an endearing, pixie grin. I had never met them before, but I knew in an instant who they were. Aunt Emmeline and Uncle Jake! My mother had called them, I was told, asking them to meet me and look after me while I was in California, so I wouldn't be alone and unprotected. They had come down to the station to meet and greet me and take me home with them to their protected space.

What a conflict! How could I hurt these dear relatives' feelings my first day in this new land? Would I be starting to "Go Hollywood" my very first day?

Mr. Boutonniere took charge. He was cordial and understanding, but explained to Mr. and Mrs. Hohn that I was expected at the CBS headquarters to meet Jesse Lasky, the producer of the Gateway to Hollywood show. After the interview, he would deliver me to the Studio Club, sponsored by the YWCA, he told them, guessing wisely YWCA would be reassuring to them. I could call them when I got there.

I was grateful and relieved. But also a little sad leaving and disappointing two dear people with whom I had at least some connection. We had the same last name — Hohn, long O. Even their slight German accents were familiar. My father had had a heavy one.

So I sped off with my new host to the CBS building. On the way I saw hills, and way up, near the top, a huge sign that sent a shock wave through me from head to heart to toe. HOLLYWOOD was strung in metal letters across hundreds of feet of undergrowth. This was it! I had arrived. No turning back now. My adventure was now really about to begin.

I hadn't had time to change clothes or freshen up before I was escorted to the elevator of the CBS building and into the offices of Jesse Lasky, a prominent figure in the history of the film industry. Remembering that day, I must have looked washed out, wan and just short of pathetic.

In the outside office, my vital statistics were taken. And when I was asked my current address, of course, without a second thought, I blithely said, "1475 West Minnehaha, St. Paul, Minnesota."

That's when the first shock came. Everyone in the room, second directors, publicity men, secretaries, camera men, and others, burst out laughing! Ha! Ha! It had never occurred to me that that perfectly understandable, historic Minnesota name, Minnehaha, was funny! Hadn't they ever heard of Hiawatha and his beloved Minnehaha?

I give myself credit here. I did have a certain confidence and poise learned from both my parents, so I pushed down the nubbin of hurt and recovered enough to smile and join in their amusement. Ha! Ha! But inwardly I thought, "Oh, how awful! To be laughed at, just for coming from Minnesota. What other embarrassment is in store for me?"

The next visit was to the inner sanctum of Jesse Lasky. I was introduced to a tall, full-bodied, rather elderly man who also wore a boutonniere in his lapel.

I was invited to be seated and sank down into, not onto, a very low sofa, so low that my knees practically touched my chin. (I was a tall and willowy five-seven — then). I turned my legs sideways to keep my underwear from showing, while Mr. Lasky paced back and forth in front of me, looking down at me, a somewhat puzzled expression on his face. He started asking me questions about my interests, my life in the past, my dreams of the future.

I must have told him about my father's death in the matter-of-fact way I'd learned to keep from seeming "too emotional". I told him about my wanting to be a psychologist or a professor, or a writer; and, once in a while, I'd even thought of the stage in New York. I didn't lie; I was too naive to say the tactful, appreciative thing and tell him I'd dreamed of becoming a film star. Because I hadn't.

"If I don't win this contest," I remember saying, "I'll go back to Minnesota and finish my college education. If I do happen to win, I'll stay to make the film and then go back to Minnesota to finish my education."

When he had run out of questions to ask, he stopped pacing, looked at the other attendants in the room, seemed at a loss for words, but finally said, "Well, it does seem this young lady has a lot of character!"

What did he mean by that, I wondered. Was that a compliment, or not? Something told me that "character" was about all he could think of to say about this train-weary, washed-out, poorly dressed young lady from West Minnehaha in far-off Minnesota, chosen from all the contestants in the entire North to South section of the country. Was this all the Mid-west had to offer? I didn't know who I was anymore. I was beginning to feel as though I had left the real me at home.

I was too tired to do more than mumble something, I can't remember what. But I was grateful when Mr. Lasky held out his hand to me and said, "Well, Kathryn, it's been good to meet you. We'll see a lot more of you in the days to come. Now, I'm sure you must be tired, so you'll be driven to the Studio Club where you'll be staying, and someone will pick you up in the morning, bring you here to meet your partner from New Orleans and start your first rehearsal for the radio show Sunday at the Lux Theater on Vine Street."

What a considerate thing it was for the sponsors to pick the Studio Club that had been the setting for the film *Stage Door* with Ginger Rogers and Katharine Hepburn. It was relaxed, friendly, well protected, but with enough flexibility to accommodate the strange, irregular schedules of aspiring young film actresses and a script girl or two. Other Gateway To Hollywood contestants were there, Linda Darnell among them.

At the Studio Club I was shown to a large, homey room. I unpacked, called Aunt Emmeline and Uncle Jake to explain and apologize, read a little and started a letter home. The matron of the Studio Club had invited me to dinner. It was then, that first night, that I tasted my first avocado and was shown how to eat my first artichoke. I fell in love with them both. I'd have to tell my mother and the girls about these strange fruits. Dinner over, I excused myself, went to my room, changed clothes, and fell into bed, sniffling a bit from relief that the first day in Hollywood was over. Only twenty-one more days, and I could go home — to 1475 West Minnehaha, where I understood (almost all the time) what was going on, how I was supposed to behave, what was funny — what was not. I punched my pillow, tossed and turned, prayed a frantic prayer, "Dear God, help me," and finally fell asleep.

⤜⤚ *Chapter Three* ⤙⤛

THE NEXT DAY. Oh, the next day! That, more than any other happening,
led me on to The Road Less Traveled. I dressed in one of my borrowed
blue dresses. On my way to the studio in the CBS building, I saw my first oleanders, hibiscus, palm trees and jacaranda. They were beautiful, but not the
pine and birch and wild roses that looked and smelled, "Home!"

When I walked into the rehearsal room at the CBS building, three men rose
to greet me, mature men, the director of the radio show, the writer, and another man. This other man bowed a little in a gentlemanly way and drew out
a chair for me.

The director introduced himself and then nodded to the Other Man.

"Kathryn Hohn, meet your partner, Mr. Hugh Beaumont, from New Orleans,
Louisiana. Hugh, meet your partner from Minnesota."

"This man!" I thought. "This *older* man? My partner?" Handsome in a rug-
ged sort of way. But so much *older!* Not a college boy. Not what I was used
to — or expected.

Thank goodness for the bit of poise that covered my disappointment.

"I'm pleased to meet you," I lied.

"The pleasure is mine," he answered, also lying, as I was to learn later. He
drew out a chair for me.

Weeks later I learned, as we laughed together, what thoughts his gracious lie
had covered.

"My God," he had thought. "A child! From where? Minnesota? That must
be somewhere north of the Mason-Dixon line — the Upper Midwest. Maybe
that's why she has straw in her hair!"

What a way to begin a relationship.

During the rehearsals, I learned that Hugh was a far more experienced and
competent actor than I. I had done one radio show, a fifteen-minute com-
mercial for the Betty Bree cosmetic company, now defunct. For three or four
weeks I had gotten thirteen dollars for fifteen minutes and thought I was
not only experienced, but rich. I had even bought my mother a toaster for
Christmas with money I'd saved.

Hugh had co-written, directed, and acted in a radio show in Long Beach,
California, and studied and acted for years at the Long Beach Community

Theater under the direction of Elias Day. This fine Little Theater provided Hollywood with such prominent actors as Robert Mitchum, Dean Jagger, and Laraine Day. Recently, Hugh had been actor-director of Federal Theater in New Orleans. The Gateway To Hollywood contest was an avenue for him to return to California, nearer his mother and young sister; and, it would, he hoped, provide an opportunity to break into film.

I was delighted with my twenty-five dollars a week from Gateway, my chance to earn some college tuition money and return to Minnesota.

It soon became clear to me that Hugh was also much wiser and more experienced in the "ways of the world" than I. We were thrown together a lot during those first days, preparing for the radio show, appearing at dinners for the Gateway participants, screen tests, rehearsals and interviews for the press. During that time, more than differences began to emerge. Hugh liked ideas, as did I. He liked to discuss everything from politics to religion, and in this I believe he found me a lively partner.

As a matter of fact, one day he said to me. "I never would have thought I'd find myself so interested in an eighteen, going-on-nineteen-year-old young lady."

I was highly flattered. A far cry from the Midwestern "child with straw in her hair."

During those first days, Hugh, with his archetypal fatherliness, took on the role of Father-Protector for me, a much needed and longed-for role since the illness and death of my own father.

One free day, he invited me to the Hollywood Men's Club for a swim and to lunch afterward. I was delighted. I was an excellent swimmer, having spent my summers since babyhood on a lake in Northern Minnesota. This was an opportunity for me to show off one of my skills. I had no idea he was eager to see, not how well I could swim, but how I looked in a bathing suit! No big deal. There were ten thousand lakes in Minnesota. Everyone wore bathing suits. Everyone swam!

That lunch day, during dessert, Hugh very gently asked me if I'd ever thought of wearing high-heeled shoes? I hadn't really thought of that anyone noticed my footwear. Saddle shoes and bobby sox were the "in" thing, even in sub-zero weather. I had one pair of little black flats for dress-up.

But now I was embarrassed, and even though Hugh could not see them now, I tucked my flat-heeled shoes under my chair to hide my shame.

"Why, no," I answered, " My mother hasn't wanted me to wear high-heeled shoes, because she has bunions, you see, and they hurt her so much and she thought high-heeled shoes caused bunions."

Hugh grinned as he continued. "Well, you see," he informed me, "high-heeled shoes make a woman's legs look long and beautiful. You'd look good in them. Why don't you try a pair?"

Thus ended my first wardrobe lesson in Hollywood. I learned to wear, walk in, even run, in high-heeled shoes, and subsequently developed painful bunions.

The big day of the radio show came and went. Each episode included a star, and the star in our show was Boris Karloff of Frankenstein fame. This tall, dignified actor was my first introduction to the great variety of personalities there were in Hollywood. Mr. Karloff was a gentleman in every way. Frankenstein's monster spoke no word aloud, so one could not have known Mr. Karloff had a beautiful, deep voice with an English accent and a slight lisp, very slight. He was a devoted gardener and raising "rotheth" was his specialty.

The script itself was not great and didn't exactly bring out the real possibilities in either Hugh or me. But I got through both the show and my astonishment at the crowd outside the theater waiting for autographs. I'm nobody, I thought. But I signed anyway and realized later that maybe they thought I might be Somebody, some day!

Neither Hugh nor I won the contest. I felt a bit let down, but also strangely relieved. I did wonder how my classmates and professors at Hamline, and my mother, of course, would feel. Would they be disappointed in me? I had no idea who had voted for me, if anybody. But I was both pleased and a little jealous that my partner, Hugh Beaumont, had won the attention of one of the greatest of Hollywood producer-directors, Cecil B. DeMille, who had been on the panel for the radio show and had voted for Hugh.

Aunt Emmeline and Uncle Jake were in the audience, of course, and offered their sweet solace; but they were quick to reassure me that my losing was "probably best," since a Hollywood career didn't seem quite right for me, somehow. Now I could go back home and continue my education, first and highest on Father's list of life-goals for me.

The next day as I was starting to pack for home, I got a call from RKO studios asking me to come to the studio to meet Gregory La Cava, a very prominent director (the one who had directed Stage Door), the popular film that

CBS Gateway to Hollywood, March 5, 1939
Hugh Beaumont, Ken Nile (announcer), Kathryn Hohn,
Jesse L. Lasky, Boris Karloff

In those first days, lots of picture-taking. My smile here is genuine. I loved
gardenias *and* Mr. Karloff. "Rothes" from him were in my dressing room.

had used the Studio Club as a model for the setting). Seems this famous man wanted to meet with me!

I walked the mile from the Studio Club to RKO. It honestly didn't occur to me to call a taxi. I had never hired a taxi in my entire life. When I arrived, hot and tired, I was escorted to La Cava's suite and, fortunately, offered a chair farther from the floor than the sofa in Jesse Lasky's office.

A bronze-faced man, slight, not too tall, greeted me with a warm, wry grin.

"I can't believe you lost that contest, Kathryn. I was one of the judges and voted for you. Found out later the contest had been rigged and RKO already had the winner under contract. The bastards! Nobody is going to use 'me like that and get away with it. So, I asked to see you here. What are your plans now?"

I blinked a bit at his unfamiliar language, but then, quickly I told him my plan was to go back home to Minnesota and finish my education.

"Interesting," La Cava said, turned away from me, and looked out the window.

Turning back to face me, he said, "How would you like to stay here and be in a film I'm preparing with Ginger Rogers? *Fifth Avenue Girl* I think I'm calling it."

Just like that! Was this confused state going to go on forever?

"Well, I — I'm not sure. I — "

Another voice broke in, a publicity man, or the studio casting director, I had no idea who. "What do you mean you aren't sure!" The same response I'd heard in Minnesota when the call from the RKO distributor first came.

I squirmed in my seat. "Well, you see, I promised my father before he died I'd finish my education."

Silence in the room. This was just like the telephone conversation in Minnesota. I was getting the message. My casualness about this astonishing offer was shocking. How could anyone be so hesitant about such an opportunity? How many thousands of young women in the whole USA would swoon at this chance, one's first part in a major film with a major director!

It was La Cava himself who rescued me. My response neither offended nor shocked him. His grin grew wider. "Well, Miss Minny-so-ta. Tell you what. One possibility. You can be in my film, see how you like it, and *then* go back home."

At that moment, who should walk in the door but Ginger Rogers! The star! She was bronzed and freckled from a vacation at Lake Tahoe and she had let her eyebrows grow, blond, and bushy. The focus was no longer on me, thank goodness. This was the closest I might ever be to a real star. There was lots of animated discussion about her eyebrows, which were different than the highly plucked, arched brows in vogue back then. I sat silently and listened to the conversation.

La Cava liked her eyebrows and I must say I did too. She looked natural, and "outdoorsy", and she'd been vacationing at a *lake*, therefore, she must be a real person. There was more discussion about the upcoming film, one of Ginger's first non-dancing movies, and I was forgotten.

When Ginger left, La Cava turned back to me and said, "Kathryn, why don't you go back to the Studio Club and think about it? There'll be a part in *Fifth Avenue Girl* if you want to give it a try. RKO will undoubtedly want an option to put you under a six month contract You don't need an agent, so you won't have to pay that ten percent and you can save enough to pay for your entire college tuition."

No pressure, thank goodness. I liked Mr. Gregory La Cava very much. I'd take his advice, go back to my private room at the Studio Club and think about it.

Chapter Four

"WHAT WOULD YOUR FATHER THINK? — finish your education — don't Go Hollywood! — have an adventure — come back — place waiting — finish — seventy-five dollars a week — adventure — "

These were not real thoughts. They were voices in my head, careening around, bumping up against each other. Where were my own real thoughts and feelings? I had no idea. I didn't know where to turn to find out.

I called my mother. I called my brother, both way off in Minny-so-ta. Called Uncle Jake and Aunt Emmeline. All seemed to be as shocked as I. Who was there who knew anything about Hollywood, Hollywood contracts, options, etc? Who was there? Nobody. Nobody at all in my past life who knew anything about Hollywood — agents — stars — starlets. All they knew were shady reputations and reports of temptations powerful and devastating. "Going Hollywood" meant everything from bankruptcy to broken marriages, to drunkenness, and eventually even to suicide. If I stayed in Hollywood, would I slip-slide inevitably down into this seductive darkness?

Should I sign, or not sign? Who was there to guide and advise me? How could I possibly make such a monumental decision all alone, all by myself? I was frightened, bewildered, and very, very lonely.

That night I lay in my bed at the Studio Club, too full of bewilderment to think a single thought that made any sense. All I was aware of was a great, heavy emptiness like a black hole inside of me. Instead of being greatly complimented by La Cava's interest, and excited by his offer of a part in a major film, I was homesick!

Were my fellow choir members at this moment in time still on tour, singing their hearts out in small towns across southern Minnesota? Did they miss me as I missed them?

Nothing in my past life had prepared me for any of this, not parsonage life, not many years filled with my father's excruciating pain, not bed pans nor hypodermic needles, neither hospital visits nor Northwoods adventures — nothing in college life, singing in the choir, studying Psychology I and II, Philosophy and Ethics I and II, English Lit, college dances, well chaperoned and ending with a midnight curfew. None of this had prepared me for the Hollywood life I was now invited to enter.

Out of that emptiness, all at once, words came to me: "Out of the night that covers me . . . " — lines from a poem by Ernest Henley. It was one of the poems in my father's book, *One Thousand and One Famous Poems*. I had memorized and recited many of them for him during his long, mysterious illness. It was a wonderful little book with poetry from Emerson to Emily Dickinson. Memorizing from it was the beginning of my lifelong love of poetry for which I have been forever grateful. I memorized quickly, and my father was proud of me for this gift. He would sometimes join me in those poems he had also memorized, and our togetherness in this shared experience brought him a bit of surcease from his incredible pain. Now, in my mind, I heard his voice, deep, mellow:

> *Black as a pit from, pole to pole.*
> *I thank whatever gods may be,*
> *for my unconquerable soul.*

What would my father think? What would he want me to do? He was not here to tell me now. He had died, saying only this to me in his dying days: "I am not afraid to die. But I am sorry I cannot live to see you finish your education."

"Finish your education. Finish your education." As I struggled to get some sleep, my father's words kept returning, and with the words came memories that did not seem significant but intruded themselves in my mind, and I could not push them away.

Something in me still did not want to dip down into into the darkness of my past. Too much pain — too much shame? But now, surrounded by strangeness, with nothing around me that was known, my past unreeled in my mind, frame by frame. It was as though I had no control over the camera and the unreeling of my story. My past, now, had a life of its own.

To my great surprise, it was not a vision of my father's face that came to me first, but an almost forgotten memory of my mother. I had kept a snapshot of her in a little box, for some reason unclear to me. There she is, in a bathing suit, sitting on the edge of our old wooden boat pulled up on the shore of the lake at our summer place in northern Minnesota. She is overweight, my fat Mama, of whom I was sometimes ashamed, who irritated and frustrated me at every turn, it seemed. There is an angry scowl on her face, squinting into the sun, holding her long, glorious hair away from her eyes. In this photo her hair looks stringy, heavy, wet from the lake bath she has most likely just taken. That hair was something that had to be taken care of, unbraided, combed, re-braided every day.

Remembering, I see her now enacting this daily ritual. She is sitting in front of her vanity dresser mirror, undoing her braid. She has brought the braid around in front of her. When the braid is undone, she combs it gently, carefully, using a yellowed ivory comb with far-apart teeth. Slowly, carefully, she combs down to the very end. More carefully still, she works apart the entwined ends that had held the braid together. She takes little batches of combed-out hair and tucks them neatly into an ivory box with a hole in the top. Combing completed, she lifts the great, burnished-brown cascade from her lap and lets it fall from her lap, crackling with life. It touches the floor. She lets it hang there for a moment, soberly looking at herself in the mirror before she reaches back, pulls the glory around in front of her, finds three equal strands with her fingers, and starts to weave them into a braid again. Then she deftly pins the braid around her head like a crown.

I do not see myself in this memory. But I must have been there often to remember it so well. I must have watched silently, absorbing each detail, knowing without thought or word, as children do, that I was sharing a sacred ritual.

This remembered scene awakened another memory, this time of a recurring childhood nightmare.

The Dream

I am a child. I am running down a street in a foreign village. The streets are cobblestone as in a German fairy-tale village. I am running away from some pursuer, the persistent robber of childhood nightmares. I run and run, never gaining ground, until a manhole in the middle of the street suddenly appears, and into it I fall — down — down — down, like Alice in the rabbit hole. As I descend, I am slowly aware of different levels. Terrible things are happening on each level. Now, I can only remember the deepest, final level. My mother is sitting in a barber chair. My father is standing silently behind her. She is having her hair cut, bobbed, as the current usage stated it. Seeing that happening is absolutely terrifying and grief-producing. I watch helplessly in horror and anguish. I wake up sobbing.

A Very Early Memory

I am alone. Crying. I am standing in my crib with wooden bars almost as high as I am. It is dusky inside the room, but outside it is still daylight.

I hear the voices of my Mama and some other woman talking, laughing, into Life, and I am left alone in my crib, "because it's bedtime," Mama said, even though it is daytime.

How can Mama leave me here, out of Life, out of belonging, and they out there in the day, on the sidewalk between our house and the church?

I shake the wooden bars that fence me in and leave me alone, angry, help-less, lost and lonely. I long to be out there with them, held in Mama's arms, up where the faces are.

My Mama does not hear me. Or, if she hears me, I am ignored. I am left to handle my grief and my rage all by myself.

After so long, so very long a time, I give up the struggle. My tears have been useless. I sit down, then lie down, curl up, and finally fall asleep.

Another Early Memory

I am small. My Mama is huge — a huge, round being way up high in a chair at the table, a long way above me.

Way up there, Mama is still slowly eating and drinking coffee. I have slid down off my place at the table, freed from the food I am too excited to eat. I haven't finished my lunch. That is not good, I know, but Mama says nothing. I couldn't stand the stiffness of the table, the chair, the messiness of my plate, half filled with food.

Other, more important things are going to happen — soon. I am going to a party, a birthday party! It is to be my first.

I am excited. So young to be going to a party. I have a new dress of challis, a fine, soft wool of the palest pink with pink pearl buttons on the shoul-ders.

I have a present to give, all wrapped in tissue paper. There will be cake and ice cream I was told, and best of all *other children,* a fact of great im-portance to me, so much younger than my two brothers and with no chil-dren in the neighborhood.

Waiting until party time is hard enough. To eat food that was not ice cream is impossible. So I slide off my seat with a swift " 'scuse, please," and start to go up to my room to put on my pink challis dress before Mama can stop me and insist *I finish my lunch!"*

"Katya," Mama calls from the great distance above me at the table, "go upstairs, take off your dress and get in bed. You need to take a nap before the party."

It cannot be! A nap? Years of waiting in bed before the party? How can I sleep at a time like this!

Nubbins of rebellion push at me.

"I don't need a nap!"

"Yes, my dear, you need a nap, especially before a party. So you won't get too tired."

"I won't get too tired!" How can she know what I need?

"Yes, you will. Now don't argue with your mother. Go on up to bed before I have to carry you up. And go to the bathroom before you lie down. You need to wee-wee."

This is too much. "No, I don't!" I have to know something about myself she doesn't know. But I feel the pressure where the pee comes out. I put my hands between my legs to keep it from pouring out beyond my control.

Still, I insist. "I don't have to wee-wee!"

"Katya, you do. Now, go on!" Sternness oozes from her and solidifies.

Nubbins inside me turn to shoves. I feel steeliness rise and force out the shout, "Shut up!"

Where had I heard those terrible words? My brother, who was always getting into trouble? I start to tremble as fear and pee fall down my legs in a warm and awesome trickle. What have I done? What did I say? I'd peed on the floor and said "shut up" to my mother. What was coming next? I am paralyzed. I just stand there, waiting. Mama had never spanked me before in my whole life. But now?

Mama is completely silent. She simply sits there and finishes her coffee. Life slows down to a solemn throb as I wait, rooted to the floor, my legs and socks wet, a puddle of pee at my feet.

After an eternity, my large, round Mama rises from her chair, takes my hand, calmly, but firmly. "You're going upstairs to bed, young lady, wash yourself and go to bed. Young ladies who say 'shut up' to their mothers do not deserve to go to parties."

Time slows down in fear and shame, then falls into nothingness. I have defied my mother. My punishment is to be forever banished from party homes that only perfect, good girls could enter.

I lie in bed obediently for a long time, sleepless, tearless. When I thought the party surely must be over, I hear my father come home, hear the muted sounds of my parent's conversation. I couldn't hear the words that were spoken.

When, at last, my father comes into my bedroom and sits on the edge of my bed, he looks deeply into my eyes and calmly, gravely asks, "Are you aware how unkind you were to your mother — she who has cooked and cleaned and cared for you day after day, made clothes for you, tucked you in bed at night, sang to you?"

Gravely, I nod my head, shame pouring through me, warmer than the pee that had puddled at my feet.

"Thank you," says my father. "I am hurt and surprised that you, my dear daughter, could act that way. I trust this kind of thing will not happen again. I'll leave you now to think about how you have behaved." He leaves the room and closes my door gently. I hear voices coming from my parents' bedroom, too soft for me to hear what was said.

My mother comes in and tells me to get dressed. I put on my beloved pink dress and pick up my beautifully wrapped gift. My father takes me to the party. I don't remember anything about it. What I did remember was that my mother had almost robbed me of my very first children's party.

Chapter Five

WAS THIS THE INCIDENT that made me fully aware of my father? Was it his interceding for me and taking me to the party?

Until some vague childhood time, my mother was the being who was always there. She was a kitchen, food and sewing person, there to help me dress, to comfort, feed and scold me.

My father was more of an idea than a solid human being. He was gone much of the time. He was somewhere out in the wider world beyond the cozy known of my house, my mother, my bed. Me inside my home was all there was.

There came a time, however, when out of the mists of undefined oneness with my mother, other beings began to take shape. There were two brothers, gone much of the time also, one eight years older than I, always getting into trouble; the other, the hero, was thirteen years older. Then, most vividly, my father emerged, he of great stature and deep voice.

This man, "my Daddy", was almost always home for the evening meal, called supper in our house. It was he who reminded us to bow our heads, fold our hands and say the blessing together, "God-is-great-and-God-is-good-and-we-thank-Him-for-our-food" in sing-song voices that helped me to remember the words.

It was he who picked me up, patted me gently, soothing my screams, when I stuck my finger into an open electrical socket. It was he who carried me in his arms, stunned and bleeding, when I hit the back of my head on the cement steps trying to turn a somersault on the iron railing.

When this Daddy was at home, other than at mealtimes, it seemed he was always in his study, except on Saturday mornings when he helped Mama roll out noodle dough or beat the eggs whites for angel food cake. This study was a special sanctuary, a sacred space. The door was always closed, no one could even knock on the door if Father was inside. I could only hear his deep voice talking to a visitor, or talking on the telephone, the only one in the house.

That study fascinated me. When my father was not at home, and the door was open, I could cautiously enter into this sacred space. Perhaps there I could find something that would bring him closer to me.

There was a huge stand in the corner with an enormous, always open book on it. The book had tissue paper pages and pictures of flags and strange animals and a naked man and woman on either side of a tree with a snake wound round its trunk. Once in a great while, when my father was in his study, I was allowed to step on the foot stool in front of the book and feast my eyes, and turn the pages, if I was very, very careful.

But the holy of holies, the untouchable mountain, was the top of my father's desk. There, I was not allowed. I couldn't reach it anyway. However, there was a chair in front of the desk that went round and round. The sun shone through the window over my father's desk and tiny coins danced in the column of light above it. Surely, these were treasures that could be caught and held, if I could only reach them.

On the long ago day I was now remembering, I was drawn to that desk by the lure of its mystery. Something of my father, some special Something, was on that desk top besides the dazzling coins. If I could reach that Something, maybe I could draw him closer to me.

I must have struggled to still the swiveling chair long enough to use as a stepping-stone to the wondrous plateau above me. I barely remember the struggle. I clearly remember sitting on top of the desk. At last I was close enough to grasp a handful of those shimmering golden coins, close my fingers around them, and have them be all mine.

I remember reaching out in ecstasy and triumphantly closing my hand around as many as my small fingers could hold. Slowly, I opened my palm. Nothing there. Nothing. Just as many dancing coins were swirling around in front of me as before. Not one was in my hand. How could this be? How could something be nothing? I could not seize and hold that glory that somehow belonged to my father. I could only look at my empty hand with grief and wonder.

Other mysteries, however, abounded on the desk; and because my father was gone and my mother was rattling around in the kitchen, I knew this was my time for further exploration. Close at hand, I saw the magic stick my father used to make scratches on paper. I saw a small silver thing along its side. It needed to be explored. And was. It moved. But to my horror, when I managed to lift the silver sliver, black drops fell from the tip and landed on my dress. I tried to brush it off. That only made it worse. It seemed to be there to stay.

Now, twin feelings of fear and dismay washed over me. What to do? This was my most beloved blue dress my mother had made and embroidered yellow daisies on. I was frantic. I searched the top of the desk for something, some way to make good my mistake before my mother found out. I saw a pair of scissors lying there. I knew what they were. Mama used scissors in her sewing.

I was just learning to cut with my own blunt-ended pair. These scissors were big, with pointed ends. I could cut out the dark blob on my dress. My problem would be solved.

This was not easy. Large scissors, small hand. But I finally made it. I cut out, as carefully as I could, around the black blob. Horror followed my work! A hole! A hole bigger than the black blob. An empty space that could not come out. With that discovery, my confusion, fear and failure were complete. I broke into wails of despair.

That's when my mother came running, saw me on the desk top, saw the fountain pen, the scissors. Had I cut myself? Was I hurt?

Yes, I was terribly hurt, hurt and frightened, as I pointed to the hole in my beloved blue dress.

My mother saw the hole, saw my heart break and horror and swept me into her arms to comfort me. Together, then, we examined the dress and when my sobbing became more quiet, she soothed me, "Don't cry, Katya. Know what we'll do? We'll sew a patch over the hole, and I'll embroider a daisy over it and nobody will notice."

And she did.

I, however, never felt quite right about that dress. It wasn't perfect anymore. Even if nobody else noticed the patch, I knew it was there. What I forgot, until this moment, was that my mother, with calm and reason — and love — had tried to make my appalling mistake as nearly perfect as possible.

"Please don't tell Daddy," I sniffled.

"It's our secret," my mother said, and kissed the top of my head.

Out of the swirling fog of childhood it slowly dawned on me that there was a world beyond home, and that world belonged to my father. It was he who set it in motion and kept it running.

Before learning to count on my fingers, or name the days of the week, I learned there was something different about one day, one block of existence between waking in the morning and going to bed at night. All the rest of the days led to that special time.

As both my mother and father rolled out noodle dough and spread the thin sheets all over the kitchen, and father returned to his study and shut the door to do some mysterious work, I came to realize that all this busyness was leading to a piece of time that was very, very important. That piece had a name, and its name was Sunday.

And in that Sunday, my father walked, with me skipping beside him, my hand in his, to the place that was the center of the world. That place also had a name. And its name was Church.

After taking me to a room with other children for something called Sunday School, my father walked away. The next time I saw him, I was sitting beside my mother in a great, high-ceilinged room with a many-colored window that the light shone through, illuminating the figure of our dear Jesus, tenderly holding a lamb in his arms. There, beneath the figure of Jesus, way up high above us, standing alone in front of us and all the many, many people around us, was my father, the Center of the Center. And my heart knew great feelings I later learned were awe, wonder — and pride.

In that dark night, years away from my long ago childhood, and far from home, these memories kept me tossing and turning. I was exhausted, but sleep was impossible. I turned over in my bed again, hugged my pillow as close as I could get it, and imagined I was holding close all those back home who loved and understood me, and gradually the heaviness eased. I turned over again and stared at the ceiling in the dimly lit room. As I stared, another long ago memory began to emerge from the black pit that overwhelmed me. The fears, confusions and loneliness faded. Slowly I began to smile all by myself, in the dark.

I see myself as a child of four-going-on-five. I am in this church, my father's church, the Methodist Episcopal Church in New Ulm, Minnesota, my birth home. Just a few Sundays ago my mother had decided I was old enough to sit by myself in the front row of the sanctuary. I wanted to be as close as possible to my father.

From my small space, I watch the towering man in the pulpit far above me. I watch every move he makes. He is standing there, tall and stately, with the light from the stained glass window above the altar shining down on him, like a holy halo. He is holding a hymnal in one hand.

"We will now rise and join in singing our closing hymn, number so and so," he announces in his deep bass voice. I watch him lift his arms wide, inviting the congregation to stand.

I don't understand the words of the sermon, but I love to sing, and when my father announces this closing hymn, I stop swinging my legs back and forth, stop dreaming about the Sunday afternoon funny papers at home, and obey my father with the rest of the congregation, as we rise raggedly to our feet.

I know by the organ's first notes that this is my favorite hymn.

"Jesus calls us o'er the tumult," I sing, loud as I can, screeching almost, still hearing the deep bass voice of my father rising above all the rest. "Of our lives, wild, restless sea" — down to the part I understand and love the most.

"Saying, Christian, follow me!"

"Yes, oh, yes, my father, whose name is Christian, for whom our religion was founded, and for whom this church was built, I will follow you all the days of my life, and I will dwell in the House of the Lord, the house that was built for you, forever! Amen!"

Another story was kept alive for me by my mother. "We had moved to Warrenton, Missouri," my mother told practically everybody to my childhood embarrassment, "where Katya's father had taken a job to raise money for an orphanage there. He was gone our very first Sunday in Warrenton, so I took Kathy to church with me. And it happened to be communion Sunday, you see, and since the Methodist church has open communion, the minister invited all those who professed the Christian faith to come forward to the altar to receive Holy Communion. And all the people came forward, row by row, and knelt at the altar, and that's when Katya leaned into me and whispered, 'How come all these people know Daddy?' I was so tickled! I tried to explain it all to her, but it wasn't easy. I told her to ask her daddy when he came home. I don't know if she ever asked him or not."

I didn't tell my father for a long, long time how mixed up I was about his relationship with the Christian religion. His name was, indeed, Christian, so how was I suppose to know that Christians were more than just the people who followed my father? I only knew I worshipped him. And so did a lot of other people, it seemed to me.

Years later when I finally did tell him about my confusion, he hugged me, and laughed with tears in his eyes until he had to blow his nose, his big nose. Would he hug me and laugh at my confusion now? I longed to know; but comforted by this warm memory, calm came over me, and — I fell asleep, without tossing and turning.

"Finish your education. Finish your education." A few nights before I made my decision about signing an RKO contract, I heard these same words again and again. They came like a solemn litany and with the words came wave after wave of painful memories I had so forcefully pushed deep down inside me to keep from feeling the agony of grief.

After my father's death, I had schooled myself not to feel the pain, with admonitions from well-meaning parishioners not to grieve, to be brave, to be grateful that my father was now relieved from his suffering.

But now, far from home, painful scenes from the darkest days of my shroud-ed past mingled with the longing for home and unreeled in my mind, frame by frame. Each frame had a life of its own. I could no more stop them than I could have stopped the crashing waves of the ocean. I turned over in my bed and pulled the pillow over my head. But the scenes continued unreeling, and I helplessly gave in to their power. Now, I felt, in every bone and sinew of my body, the hopeless and despair I had suppressed for years.

⤚⟶ *Chapter Six* ⟵⤙

IT ALL SEEMED TO HAVE BEGUN WITH THE GREAT DEPRESSION, when I was still a child. The Crash burst in on us in 1929 when we were still living in Minneapolis. With the shock of walls tumbling down faster than Jericho's, and bodies falling through the air, depression came to our house to stay. Now we had no money. None. After the bills were paid, there was nothing left to buy a new dress for me, or drapes for my mother, or send my errant brother to aviation school, which he so longed for.

I heard things. "People can't pay their pledges. So and so lost his job, can't find work, can't pay the rent."

I want something. Perhaps just one doll that cries "Mama" when you tip her over.

My father takes me on his lap, and with his arms circling round me, he opens a little book in front of us. "This is our check book," he says, slowly, carefully. "This is where I put down the amount of money we have in the bank. After the bills are paid, I subtract that amount from our money in the bank. And this is what is left over."

I look, my heart beating with fear. $9.36.

"So you see," my father says, "that's all there is to buy food and pay for the coal we need to keep us warm. Much as I would like to, I cannot buy it for you."

I slide down off his lap in terror, shame, confusion. I stop asking for things.

That fall, in Crookston, Minnesota, in the Red River Valley of the North, where we had moved after our short stay in Minneapolis, the results of the Great Depression deepened. Hungry men came daily to our back door looking for a way to earn a meal. My mother kept a table set for them in our enclosed porch. There were hoboes in our parks, breadlines in the streets of cities and towns, despair in every corner of the country.

It hurt my father deeply to pay the farmer only nine cents a dozen for eggs. He took produce in place of cash for pledges to the church.

We watched the papers for falling prices — fifteen cents a pound for hamburger — twelve cents — ten cents — what would the bottom be? When would it come?

There were letters in the paper and cries from everywhere, "Why doesn't the government do something about it?"

The reality that made it all possible to bear was that we all seemed to be in it together, from the highest to the lowest, even we children; sometimes especially us, who felt even more helpless than the grown-ups.

But, in our own household, a deeper depression hung like a pall over us; me, my mother and especially, my father.

I am lying in bed in my pink bedroom, not able to sleep, wondering what I can do to make things better. Across the hall in another bedroom, my father is lying alone, his door closed tightly. I wait in fear for what I know is sure to come.

After some time, it begins — low groans at first, then rising in intensity as the moments tick by. It is not long before I hear my mother's footsteps crossing the hall to open the door to my father's room. With the opening of the door, the deep, rising, guttural groans of my father seem to shake the house and fill the world. I get out of bed to join my mother and stand beside her as we watch helplessly at the foot of my father's bed.

There he lies, his face contorted in agony, twisting and turning, pulling mightily on the brass bedposts until they quiver, crying aloud, "Ach mein Gott in Himmel — oh, my God, my God, help me, please help me!"

What can I do to help this tortured man? If his pleas to the Almighty to relieve his agony are not answered, what use would my childish whimpering be? I cannot even touch my father. The slightest fingertip caress and he would cry out, "Nein, nein! No! No! Bitte! Please! Oh, go, please!"

I cling to my mother and wait in silence for our kind, but equally bewildered doctor to answer my mother's call and administer a powerful pain-killer so that we, all three, could get some sleep .

While we were still living in Minneapolis, my father had gone to the Mayo Clinic in Rochester for a diagnosis, but at that time no one in that distinguished institution could find the source of his slowly, but steadily increasing pain.

It seemed to have started when he was traveling with a bus load of orphans here and there all over the state of Missouri to raise money for Central Wesleyan Orphanage. Having the children along, to sing, to answer questions, enhanced his efforts.

One day, on a return trip to Warrenton, the bus that was carrying him and the children broke down, and the driver pulled over to stop. My father walked out into the middle of the road, waving his arms to flag down a Yellow Way bus that was barreling along. The Yellow Way bus slowed down, trying to stop, but it had hit him, knocking him over. His back had been injured and he had some pain, but the doctors had felt that with time, his back would heal.

Now, several years later, each week, each day, the pain had escalated, and every single night when lying on his back, his guttural, heart-rending cries of agony shook the house and sent both mother and me hurrying helplessly to his bedside. This grueling, nightly agony had gone on for days, weeks — six years. Our beloved Dr. Hodgson finally gave my father a special hypodermic needle so he could administer his own pain killer, trusting that he would not overdose.

My father used that needle as sparingly as he could, but on Sunday, not able to get through the service without the pain-killer, he preached sitting down in the pulpit chair and said the faces of the congregation below him were blurred, indistinct as disembodied ghosts. And yet he spoke clearly, without hesitation, and no one but my mother and me knew he was on morphine.

He continued his ministry, in spite of the pain, teaching, preaching, attending meetings, visiting shut-ins, walking to town every day with his cane and stopping by merchants and other places of business to bring greetings, and wish them well.

I have two small boxes of sermons my brother Roland passed on to me. They are outlined, in English, on three-by-five, six-holed notepaper in tiny handwriting that looked like German script. "The Meaning of Suffering", "Science and Religion," "Why Do Good People Suffer?" "Dawning," (Easter Sunday's sermon) and the one I love the most, "Stewards of Mystery."

These are the subjects of sermons my father preached to his incredulous congregation. They were the subjects of conversation in our house with visitors, townspeople outside the church, and even, several times, a Catholic priest! My father loved the company, the intellectual exchange. It kept his mind off the pain, which was there everyday, but most powerfully at night, in bed, lying on his back.

After one night of unremitting agony and Father's cries of pain, my mother and I got no sleep at all. Mother shared these awesome episodes with trusted and deeply concerned parishioners and after that, faithful men of the church came to the house every night and kept vigil by my father's bedside, administering his pain killers, so mother and I could sleep the night through. Somehow, we learned to live with it. Bottles of alcohol and hypodermic needles were as common as dish pans.

What were my father's prayers, his Job-like probings and challenges as he lay down alone, trying to understand the mystery of human suffering. Did h say to himself, like Job, "Though he slay me, yet will I trust him?" I prayed, I prayed, to a God I was not sure I believed in, to bring healing to my father, to help me become a better and better person so that I would never, ever cause my father any more suffering.

In the daylight hours, there were many offerings of solace from all around the city of Crookston, Minnesota — lots of custard, soup, offerings of foot massages. But in the longest midwinter nights, we were alone, we three, suffering father, attending mother and adolescent daughter. Cousins, aunts and uncles lived in far away Nebraska or Colorado, and even one in California. Roland, my hero brother, was still away, at school. My younger brother, the troubled one, I did not know.

Late one night I was called from my bed to go into my father's room. A man was standing at the window with his back to me. I thought it must be one of the parishioners who had been called upon to stay with my father. When I came into the room, the man turned around and faced me with a warm smile and open arms. It was my brother Roland! My hero had come to rescue me. My joy and relief were boundless. Had I not realized until that moment how burdensome our life had been? Recently, after weeks, months, years of unremitting pain, my father had discovered strange lumps all over his body. He was scheduled to go down to the University of Minnesota Hospital for exploratory surgery. Mother was to go with him. Roland was called from his pre-med studies at the University of Minnesota to come home and stay with me.

We stayed together in the big, cold parsonage for an unremembered length of time. He filled in as minister for my father, and it was during that time he made his career decision to shift from medicine to the ministry.

Then, in the midst of those days, a call came from our mother at the hospital, telling us that the specialists had found, unbelievably, the source of my father's pain! It had been discovered by a resident, Dr. Howard Vogel of New Ulm, my birth home. He had come across a paragraph in a medical text he was studying and ran across a description of a disease called Von Recklinghausen's Disease. A two-inch fibroid tumor had been pressing against the sciatic nerve in the ¡ddle of my father's back. This large tumor was more than enough to cause ˙˙ting, unendurable pain, especially when he lay on his back at night. A ˙ ᡳangerous surgery was performed, the tumor removed, and the ˙ Dr. Christian G. Hohn could return to his parish and his .! Now, at long last, we were all free!

, the whole town as well, rejoiced in the news and celebrat-

· ed the miracle of modern medicine finding the mysterious cause of so much pain. Members of the congregation, as well as other townspeople in Crookston, collected one hundred dollars, a significant sum in those days. They changed the dollar bills into freshly-minted silver coins and placed them in a sterling silver pitcher inscribed with lines from *The Vicar of Wakefield*.

> In his duty prompt at
> Every call
> He watched and wept, he
> pray'd and
> felt for all
> He tried each art, reproved each dull delay
> Allured to brighter worlds
> and led the way.
> Crookston, Minnesota
> Rev. Christian G. Hohn 1930–1935

I have the pitcher sitting on a small table in my work room, reminding me as I look at it, not only of the courage of my father, but also of the love and caring of the people of Crookston, Minnesota. The Chief of Police, not even a member of our church, drove me the three hundred miles to the Twin Cities. He waited while I visited with my father and then took me back home. Every mile of the way down to Minneapolis, I held the silver pitcher on my lap with tender awe, carefully touching the engraving.

At the University of Minnesota Hospital, my father, surrounded by attentive and admiring nurses and doctors, took the pitcher carefully from my hands. He held it, read the engraving, gazed at the silver coins, then lifted it up to his thin cheek and caressed it, tears brimming.

I felt greatly honored, indeed, to have been chosen to be a part of this holy task. In retrospect, I wonder if this moment symbolized a rite of passage for me fully into the Realm of the Father?

⌘ *Chapter Seven* ⌘

Then, in those last deep depression days, cold and darkness descended upon the earth in Crookston, Minnesota, as never before. Every day, for forty days and forty nights in 1934–35, the temperature held rigidly at thirty-five to forty degrees below zero. Iced in, iced over, we hunched about in a world ringed with polar ice and snow. A strange, circular envelope of feeble, icy light enclosed us. There were rings around the sun during the day and around the moon at night. Sky, houses, trees, snow covered ground, all looked the same. There was little difference in the light coming from the sky and the light of the frozen snow-covered earth. It all gave the effect of living in a tunnel made of ice.

As young adolescents, my friends and I walked to school through the polar tunnel, layers of clothing enveloping us, chins tucked deeply into collars, turning our whole bodies when we talked to one another, rather than expose one inch of bare flesh to the subzero temperature. We never felt the cold outside, bundled up as we were. Noses and ear tips would be frostbitten before the cold could penetrate deeply enough for us to feel anything at all. We never missed a day of school, however, if I remember rightly.

Inside our house, we struggled to keep warm, hung blankets over the hall and outside doors, stuffed cloth in the cracks around the windows, kept vigil at night with the furnace that needed stoking every three or four hours — and talked about the weather. One day at fifty-two degrees below zero, we were the coldest spot in the nation, and proud of it!

The autumn before this arctic winter, our lives had been plunged again into the dismal depths of illness and pain. We had had such hope, such release from constant immersion in the suffering of my father whose body was the battleground, the suffering of all those who loved him and watched his agony with bewilderment: "From whence did this suffering come? When would it end?" We had had some short respite from all of this.

One night I crossed the hall to go to the bathroom and my father was standing in front of the mirror, touching his cheeks, which had stayed painfully thin after his long and difficult surgery. That summer he had had difficulty digesting food, and even complained that mother wasn't careful enough about the amount of butter and mayonnaise she served him to eat. Didn't she remember that he couldn't digest mayonnaise? (He could still, miraculously, digest sauerkraut!)

I watched him silently, and then went back to bed, lying awake in sadness. I soon heard his limping foot steps come up to my door.

There is an entry in my little brown diary for that night:

Daddy told me tonight that he may have cancer.

By the time my father had the necessary examinations to confirm his self-diagnosis, and had been sent to the University of Minnesota Hospital in Minneapolis, the cancer had spread too far for surgery. The prognosis was negative, colon cancer — advanced.

The attending physicians had said to him, "Dr. Hohn, we know you would want to know the truth. You are a strong and spiritual man. Your cancer is inoperable. We have to tell you. We do not give you more than six months to live. The best thing you can do is to pack your bags and go to Florida or some place in the sun and just live it up!"

That, for my father, would not be "living it up." Though he worried about my mother and me, for him, the way to live out his life would be to continue in the work which he loved so much.

His response to the doctor's advice had a compelling pathos. "I am not afraid to die. Certainly not that way. Waiting for death in the sun. I want to die with my 'poots' on!"

My father, lover of Goethe and Schiller and Kant and Jesus of Nazareth and the Old and New Testaments, used a cowboy metaphor with a still strongly German accent.

He was riding, not a horse, but trains and buses all over the northwest corner of Minnesota, serving now as District Superintendent of the Fergus Falls District of the Methodist Episcopal Church. The Bishop had called him, and my father, partly flattered and partly challenged, had accepted. My mother was furious. Didn't the Bishop know what a sick man my father was — had been? How dare he! But my father, loyal churchman to the end, accepted against my mother's protests.

We stayed in the parsonage until a replacement for my father could be found. Then, we moved to a rented house farther from the church, farther from school, but closer to my friend, my first boyfriend. And the great winter descended.

All during those nights, we were a triumvirate again, we three. My brothers were still gone from home, never to return permanently. My oldest brother, Roland, now married, was attending seminary in Boston. My younger brother,

Win, was in and out, now here, now somewhere else, still intermittently getting into trouble, still trying to find himself and his special niche in the world, still, unconsciously carrying the family "Shadow." (C. G. Jung's term for those personified parts of ourselves we push down into the unconscious because they are not acceptable to those things we have been taught by our families, our culture.)

So Mother, Father and daughter looked after each other as best we could. The bottles of sterilizing alcohol, the hypodermic needles came out again. Mama and I helped my father occasionally with his hypos which he grew so weary of administering to himself. His skin was leathery, strung over his bones like a shroud. It stayed in place when I picked it up and thrust in the needle, and watched the bit of flesh slowly sink back into place, always too much skin for such shrunken flesh.

During those bleak days, the entire community seemed to be aware of and praised my father's courage, his heroic stand against pain. He was noble in his carriage, firm in his faith. He defied the "Forces of Darkness," he said in one of his last sermons, that drew him inexorably down into the Ground of Death. He kept his boots on, and traveled, head raised.

All those whose lives my father touched in that last year, who felt the skeleton arm beneath the forty-four double-breasted suit, were in awe. Here, indeed, was the archetypal Job, the suffering servant, living out his days in splendid courage and faith.

When he was at home, which was more and more frequently as the months went by, I played games with him, sometimes it seemed all night. We played Monopoly, a bit of chess, cribbage (15–2, 5–4), checkers, rummy. Up at the lake, he had made a crude cribbage board, which I still have, out of half a birch log, made the proper holes in it, and painted the proper lines on it with red paint. I sat by his bed and recited poetry which I frantically memorized by the pages to please him. I basked in the glow of his favor, sharing the light of the admiring community. "How like her father," they would say.

At bedtime, I would fill my little brown journal with the ups and downs of self-flagellation, stuffing my own shadow feelings and trying to become the *Mädchen Ohne Schatten* (The Girl without Shadow).

I have saved many of the letters my father wrote to me through the years. Here is one, the very last. It was written just before his complex back surgery.

University Hospital
October 6, 1935
My dearest Daughter,

For the reason that further examinations of the X-Ray pictures are to be made, my session in the operating room has been postponed for a day. It will take place tomorrow morning.

So, I will have time to think of you, my dear daughter.

Naturally, my thoughts are turning to you a great deal. You are so brave, and courageous. I know you would also like to be by my side with your mother, but your school and the gulf of distance between us makes it impossible for you to be here. I know you are with me in thought and love, and you are equally sure of my love and thought of you every passing moment.

People tell me that you have much of my spirit and characteristics. I trust that what they mean thereby is that the little good in me is also in you. If that be so, I am proud that I could contribute a small mite to your personality. God bless you, my dear daughter.

Affectionately,

Dad

Summer, 1936
Me, my mother, and my father at Epworth League summer camp, near Park Rapids, Minnesota, a day or two before his last struggle with severe pain. Our very last picture together.

Chapter Eight

Time, in that long, dark, endless winter somehow passed. We longingly looked forward to spring, for the break of ice film beneath our feet as we pushed our rubber boots down to the muddy water that had melted the day before. It was the blessed time E. E. Cummings called "mud-luscious and puddle wonderful." We rejoiced as we heard the drip of water from the eaves during the first above freezing nights, and watched the brown grass appear in patches before they started to turn a come-alive green. With excitement we waited for spring to wash away the winter-dirtied snow, held our breaths in delight at the tiny leaf buds appearing on the trees and bushes and welcomed the first dandelion, the only beloved one of the year.

Spring meant release from the eternal layering of clothes, the shodding of feet with socks and boots, all the clumsy, fattening, though warming, things. Especially, for teenage girls, it was freedom from balbriggan underwear, and best of all, it meant bare legs!

With nature's surging life came the rising of hope that our house of three could open its doors, take down its storm windows and let in the light of sun and health.

But though the days grew longer and the nights swiftly shorter, pain went on and on, and the father who was the light of our lives grew thinner, fainter, weaker each day.

We went "Up to the Lake" for one last summer together, took down the shutters, aired the stored bedding, and tried to make it as much like all other summers as we could.

We took time out to go to Epworth League Institute, the Methodist summer retreat for young people. It was there, on Sunday, the last Sunday in June 1936, that my father preached and served communion for the closing of church camp for that year.

That same afternoon, he was seized with severe pain, and the local doctor in the nearest town, Park Rapids, Minnesota, took him into his home and administered pain medication. A beautiful black woman from Mississippi, who was a dear friend of my father's, went with him. She had sung German Lieder in our home and had been a guest and leader at Northern Pine Institute. She sat by his bed and sang a spiritual in her exquisite, well-trained voice.

"Were you there when they crucified my Lord? — sometimes it makes me tremble, brother, tremble — "

Then came the day, four days later, that my father died.

He, beloved and respected Protestant clergyman, died in a Catholic hospital attended by loving nuns, our family doctor, and one parishioner. According to this man, his last words were a line from a hymn, "My God is reconciled. His parting voice I hear — "

Not my mother, neither of my brothers, nor I, were with him when he breathed his last breath. There had been no chance, after all, to say a proper "Goodbye."

My steadfast boyfriend and I had been out on the lake fishing. My father had been cleaning the fish as fast as we brought them in, every half hour or so. While we were gone, my mother reported, another severe pain seized him. He dropped the fish, clutching his chest. She had somehow maneuvered him to bed, called the doctor in the near-by town, who told her to call an ambulance. She called Joe Houske, a mortician, a trusted friend and member of the congregation in Crookston, one hundred and seventy miles away.

It seems strange, now, that neither Mother nor I thought of calling the ambulance in Grand Rapids, miles and hours closer. But, anticipating his death, Father had talked over all end-of-life arrangements with Joe. We both must have felt we were fulfilling Father's desires, and reacted to the crisis without one moment of discussion.

While we waited the hours before Joe Houske arrived, Mother sat beside my father every moment of endless time it took for Joe to arrive at our cottage in his ambulance, sirens screaming..

My father was unconscious, but still living and breathing, when we watched Joe take the stretcher out of his ambulance and unfold it. He carried my father out of the cottage in his arms, lifted him onto the stretcher and enclosed him in the ambulance, sirens still screaming. He gave my mother a swift pat on the arm and drove out of the yard and out of sight toward far away Crookston, and the familiar, trusted doctor and hospital and there.

My mother bustled to clean the cottage, put away the food. Caught in the vice-like grip of life-long habit, she felt compelled to leave everything neat and clean. She seemed unaware that habit was pulling her away from her need to be with her husband on his last journey in this mortal life. She never forgave herself.

When we got to the hospital, driving seventy miles an hour (so much in those days), we were met in the waiting room of St. Vincent's Hospital by Mother Superior.

"Oh, my dear Mrs. Hohn," she said, not touching, hands folded beneath the sleeves of her habit, empathy in her quiet voice, "he's gone. Your husband has passed away. He died about two hours ago. Please, my dear, wait here. There are friends expecting you and will come as soon as I call."

And we were taken to our home, stayed with and cared for with tenderness while blanketing denial shielded us from the overwhelming reality.

Sorrowfully, I cannot say we shared the grief, my mother and I, those first shadowy days. Only the self-absorption of adolescence can explain my actions and behavior at this time. The moment a grief-producing thought would start to rise inside my mind with the chill of finality, "I'll never see my father again," I forcefully pushed the thought away.

"You're just feeling sorry for yourself," I'd say to the me I hardly knew. My guide, my Holy Grail, was to go through this experience as bravely as my father had done with his long years of pain. Accept the banal reassurances, "Now he is freed from his suffering. Now he can be at peace. It is God's will. Rejoice!" And I accepted the praise for my courage as though it was my honest due.

Not so my mother. Stunned into silence, it was as though my father's death was totally unexpected. When reality set in and the mists of unreality rose, she came out of her self-protecting cocoon, falling into a crumpled heap of desolation. Her tears were continuous and alternated with a frantic blinking of her eyes, and a furtive looking about here and there to see if anything at all were real. As the finality of her loss assailed her, she reacted as though all of life had betrayed and abandoned her.

Years before Rabbi Liebman's *Peace of Mind*, longer still before we knew anything about the research of Kübler-Ross and her understanding of the stages of grief; and yet too modern for the wailing wall and the vocalized laments of the wake, my mother was left to grieve alone. There seemed to be no solace that could stop her.

"Really, Mother, Daddy wouldn't want you to grieve like this," I'd say aloud.

Inwardly, disloyal thoughts would plow their way into my brain. "We can throw away the bottles of alcohol, the hypodermic needles. We can smell like cookies and homemade soup and non-medicinal bath powder. We can go about our lives freed from the sounds and smells of suffering."

"Really, Mrs. Hohn," parishioners would say, "it's God's will. You mustn't grieve so. You must have faith. He is released from his suffering."

"Really, Mrs. Hohn. Dry your tears. There is an Afterlife. Christian has joined His Heavenly Father. You will meet your husband there, someday."

"Honestly, Mother, we'll be all right. We can manage. I drive, and I can balance our check book. We'll get along just fine."

And still, Mother's sturdy self went on its grieving way. In spite of all that was said to her, and all her religion was supposed to have taught her, an instinct for the natural process of grieving guided her. She curled up into a circle of bereavement and stayed there until she was ready, all by herself, to uncurl into life again.

There was a service in the Methodist Church in Crookston. The large sanctuary was filled to overflowing and the sliding door to the adjoining gymnasium had been opened and filled with bleachers to accommodate the overflow of parishioners and townspeople. There was an abundance of flowers. Rev. J. Arthur Rinkel, my father's closest friend from college days, and his wife, Tanta Lee, had driven speedily all the way from southern Minnesota to Crookston to deliver the eulogy and the closing prayer.

I had warned myself not to listen to anything. I refused to look at the casket and forced myself to "be brave!" I had asked my father to will me his garnet stick pin in a gold setting, and he had agreed. I didn't check to see if it was on his tie in the casket. I don't remember anything that was said or sung.

We buried my father in the Hohn family plot of the cemetery out in the country near Seward, Nebraska. He had planned his own service. It was held in the beautiful little country church where he had sung so lustily as a young man and where he had received his "call to the ministry."

I don't even remember the eulogy. Cousins and brothers and sisters and shirttail relatives sang and sang beautifully. There was much weeping.

Just before the benediction, a grown man whom I had never before seen broke loose from the rear of the sanctuary and ran, sobbing loudly, throwing himself across the open casket, across my father's body.

He had to be pulled away by Joe Houske. Joe had brought the casket in his hearse, and with his young fourteen year-old son, Glenn, doing most of the driving, had brought it all the way from northwestern Minnesota in the hottest summer in Nebraska history.

Later I learned that the sobbing stranger was a nephew of my father's, the child of an older sister, who had died in childbirth. My mother and father had taken the newborn infant and lovingly cared for "Little Paulie" until he was five years old, when his birth father had remarried and took him back to

Nebraska. This was a trauma for my parents and obviously for young Paulie, as well; but it was not an uncommon practice in those days. No arrangements had been made for visitation. How many, many years the trauma of tragic loss and separation stays with us. Paulie never quite resolved his, and mine went underground for many years.

I understood nothing of this at the time. I merely thought Paulie's astonishing behavior was beyond understanding. Amidst all the weeping, and the sudden drama, my mother and I both sat very still, mother tearless at last.

I forced myself again, not to look at my father in the open casket before us, not to listen to anything that was said, certainly not to watch the impossible, final moment when the casket was solemnly closed and the pallbearers came down the aisle to draw it away. I watched, instead, a fly that wanted to land on my father's nose, changed its plan, and rose in a sharp diagonal to seek the sweetness of a flower.

Only when the moment came, outside, and the casket was about to be lowered into the meaningless hole in the ground that was the waiting grave, did I nearly succumb to the urge to scream or laugh hysterically and fall with a shovelful of earth into the grave with my father. Did that precious stickpin my father promised me get buried with his lifeless body? Now, it was too late to check and see.

Did my mother sense the tension in all of me as she stood, numb and tearless beside me? How did she know that this was the moment, in all the days since my father's death that I needed her the most. She leaned toward Joe Houske and whispered something in his ear. Joe took my mother's hand. He evidently had retrieved the almost forgotten stick pin from my father's tie before the casket was finally closed and slipped it now to my mother. Mother reached for my hand, enclosed the precious jewel with my fingers and held my cold hand with her warm one. Now, silently, with bowed heads and closed eyes, without weeping or hysteria, we grieved as one.

Chapter Nine

EMILY DICKINSON SAID IT WELL. "The sweeping of the heart, the putting love away, is the solemnest of ceremonies enacted upon earth." My mother and I spent the fall of 1936 with this ritual, Mother weeping often, still; I tearless and reasonable. I had my father's garnet stick pin made into a ring and wore it on the third finger of my left hand.

The practical mother knew we had to do something to improve our financial situation, which was dire, indeed. The idea of renting a house with rentable rooms, taking in roomers and boarders, teachers perhaps, came to her as naturally as breathing. Now, she quickly shifted into high gear, and within weeks had found a perfect place, very close to one of the elementary schools and the high school. And we moved.

It was not long before all of our three empty rooms had been rented by teachers and perfect breakfasts served to a dozen or so more. Mother began, at last, to re-enter life in the role she loved the most and fulfilled so well — nourisher, provider.

At the end of my junior year of high school, an opening came at Hamline University for a house mother for an annex to the women's dorm. Mother was offered the job. There was no salary, but both my mother and I would be provided with housing, all utilities paid. The President of Hamline, Dr. Charles Nelson Pace, had promised my father that he would help see to it that I got a college education. This offer seemed one step toward the fulfillment of that promise. We moved again.

At the suggestion of a friend who was attending Hamline, I was encouraged to try and enter this college, saving me the pain of adjusting to a high school many times larger than the one I was used to; and then, after graduation, changing schools again.

I talked to the admissions director at Hamline, and he was most understanding. He offered me the opportunity to take a battery of special examinations to see if I was ready to enter college.

I swelled with pride that my marks were high enough to allow me to enter Hamline immediately. Mother was disappointed. Now, she would have to wait another four years to celebrate with me the glowing rituals of graduation, the cap and gown, the parties, the public honor, the gifts!

Hamline was heaven on earth for me. I adored college life. I honestly loved learning and felt excited about it almost every day. After a tryout, I was invited to join the exceptional Hamline choir and was cast as the lead in college plays. I also got to swim in the winter, my first experience in an indoor, heated pool.

Life in the Annex was good, too. This was now "my home." At Thanksgiving and Christmas, Mother took in stray students who could not afford to leave their part-time jobs these late Depression days and pay for the bus trips to their own homes. Mother prepared and served them traditional, delicious Thanksgiving and Christmas dinners, and we gathered around the tall, decorated balsam tree for *Bescherung*, the German word for the Christmas Eve exchange of gifts, very small gifts to be sure. My first Christmas Eve in my new home, a number of us who sang in the choir bundled up and stepped out in the night to walk in the softly falling snow, singing Christmas carols. These holiday times were my very first experience of a large "family" gathering.

During these days, I took care of the car with the help of a number of Hamline boys, helped my mother a bit, and, in a distant, disinterested way, took care of her. I did not need to think about or grieve for my father. He had never left. He was there inside me, in my way of thinking and being, in my aspirations and expectations, of myself, of all others. What real, living human beings, especially men, could ever fulfill his image? I was not the least concerned about that, then. Life was richer and fuller for me than it had been for much of my childhood and adolescence.

Then, suddenly, that totally unexpected life shift had taken place, and I found myself, not at home in St. Paul, Minnesota, but lying in bed in my room at the Studio Club in Hollywood, California, facing a life-changing decision all by myself. My cherished life at Hamline University would be relinquished. My father's heartfelt desire for me to "finish my education" would be abandoned.

The conflict within me clouded my days and kept me tossing and turning at night. Should I stay here in Hollywood and pursue a film career, or should I take flight and return home to the safe and familiar? I longed to close the camera of my mind that brought the pain and the joy of my past so close to my awareness.

How I finally reached my decision is all a blur now. One voice only stands out — Hugh Beaumont's. Over Scotch on the rocks (his, of course) and a

Seven-Up (mine, obviously) he pointed out to me how rare this kind of offer was, an opportunity, he declared, that he'd give his eye teeth for.

"I have decided to stay here in Hollywood," he said, shaking the ice in his glass, not looking at me. "I'm going to try my luck in Hollywood. I'll be here to protect you from Hollywood wolves."

He looked at me then and grinned. Wolves, I thought. What were they? In my North Country they were predators, but four-legged ones that howled at the moon. I could only guess what Hollywood wolves meant, and I shrugged off the idea. I didn't see myself as a juicy morsel for two-legged wolves. But still, Hugh would be there to inform me about certain unknown dangers, and I felt comforted. I needed fatherly protection and advice, and readily accepted all he had to offer. Did his decision to stay in Hollywood have anything to do with me? I didn't dare think it. Somehow it scared me.

So I signed the contract, reassured by knowledge of the Hayes Office that protected minors from human predators. The publicity department surrounded me with interviews, photographs, more interviews. La Cava had instructed the publicity department that there was to be *no Leg Art*. What was leg art?

When I learned that "leg art" was photos taken in a bathing suit, displaying legs and upper torsos, I didn't understand La Cava's injunction against it. My summer life for years and years had been spent in a bathing suit. It was natural that most summer snapshots of me down at the water's edge were taken in a bathing suit. Wolves, leg art? These were words of a foreign language I was learning fast. I had enough pride not to let on that I didn't know what a Hollywood wolf was, or leg art. If they had known my childhood experience of the Northwoods, they would understand.

When I was two years old, my parents bought a place on a lake in northern Minnesota. During the summer months we did what many Minnesota families did and still do. We went "Up to the Lake." For us, our "Up to the Lake" place became the most stable home a moved-about minister's family would know.

My eldest brother had been very ill with the flu during the epidemic that followed World War I. Our family doctor had said to my parents, "Take Roland up to the Northwoods in the summer. Among the pines. It will help heal his lungs."

Now my father had a real altruistic reason to fulfill a dream of owning some woods like those his family had lived and worked in, back in southern Germany. He found such a place through a parishioner in New Ulm.

This magical place was an old homestead high on a hill, overlooking

Minnesota blue water, Lake Pokegama. This lovely body of water was ringed with the deep green of pine and balsam. There were two old apple trees on the property, white birches here and there, and enchanting islands in the lake that became goals for me to swim to — Blueberry, Pumpkin Seed, Wendigo.

It was here for more than sixteen summers that my family came, and our everlasting bond with our Earth Mother was formed. It was a place of healing for us all, not just my oldest brother. It was a place of release and joy, of bare feet and sunburns, of family pranks and the card game "Rook" (Methodist bridge) and Old Maid.

Occasionally, someone would wake early enough to see the sunrise, "a ribbon at a time" as Emily Dickinson described it. In the long evenings we watched slowly, gently changing sunsets, sang "Just a Song at Twilight" around the campfire and listened to the loon's hysterical laugh or melancholy cry. And most exciting of all, we often heard the haunting, shiver-making howls of the wolves from the empty miles across the lake to the north. We watched the stars come twinkling out, the moon rise. I was allowed to stay up in August, watching for falling stars, the Perseid Showers, and often, the mysterious, constantly wavering shafts of Northern Lights.

I became especially attached to a very tall Norway Pine that lifted its imposing crown far above all the other trees on the hill below our cottage. It murmured, whirred, and gently nodded far above us in response to soft summer breezes. Long before a storm broke free, the gentle whir grew to a bough-bending roar, letting us know it was time to close the doors and windows, roll up the awnings and "center down", as the Quakers would say, inside our cozy cabin. Thus, "announced by all the trumpets of the heavens" we were ready for the onslaught. My hero brother Roland had named that Norway Prophet Pine.

I loved Prophet Pine, and felt I had a special relationship to it, finding it easier to pray to than the God who wasn't real, because I could not see, hear or touch him. (I remember my quandary about this and one day asking my father the ultimate question, "Where did God stand when he created the earth?" My father chuckled warmly and told me I was thinking of God as a human being, instead of a spirit.) Prophet Pine was real. I could touch him, put my arms not quite halfway around him, look way up high into the heaven above where God the Spirit lived. Prophet Pine, not I, could talk to that spirit.

In my deep desire to become a better and better-perfect person as I grew up, I was sure Prophet Pine could help me. And so, one day I had an inspiration. I retrieved a treasure from a Cracker Jack box, a little man with an umbrella. I must have been old enough to write, because I remember scribbling a note with a prayer that I would become a better and better person, wrapping the note around the little man, putting it in a little box, picking up a knife from the kitchen and walking purposefully down the hill to the base of Prophet Pine. I dug into the earth as best I could and buried the little man, with the prayer that he would travel up the trunk of Prophet Pine and carry my message to the unseen spirit-God above. Mission accomplished, I knew Prophet Pine would help me. I felt at peace.

It was in this long shot of my past that I met the forgotten me of my life in the Northwoods of Minnesota, the ten-year old tomboy hoyden, courageous, independent, tousle-haired, bare-footed, dirty-toed, almost-forgotten me! I needed her now, her courage, her spunk. Maybe she would stay with me in the days to come.

With help from my much older brothers, I learned to swim. I got sunburned a time or two, picked blueberries in the spruce swamp all by myself. I learned to fish and row a boat. (Only the rich had motor boats.) I went fishing by myself with fishing line wrapped around my toe as I rowed. I learned to help my father seine for minnows, and then bait my own hook with those wiggly, silvery, tiny fish. One time, with the help of a "city boy," I caught an eleven-pound Northern Pike!

The ten-year-old tomboy hoyden, courageous, independent, tousle-haired, bare-footed, dirty-toed, almost-forgotten me! The 'city boy' stands on the left.

This place in the woods was a retreat for my family and a gathering place for cars full of parishioners and far away relatives. It was a place that vibrated with goodwill and the ring of hearty laughter, especially my mother's. The family had named our place "Camp Laf–a–Lot!" and it was a place of freedom from the constraints of indoor, winter, parsonage living.

I didn't wear a dress the whole summer long, but wore hand-me-down Boy Scout shorts, or overalls.

And, as often as possible — a bathing suit!

There was quite a bit of publicity about this in those first Hollywood days, "Kathryn Adams, minister's daughter, scorns leg art." And there I would be, all of me, in a bathing suit. I should have been embarrassed, I suppose, but I soon learned that publicity men, and a few women, were out for a good story, not to hurt an innocent Minnesotan. I was even respectful and fond of one journalist, Frederick Othman, would wrote a story about me, twisting my feelings about Leg Art and privacy. In that story, I sounded innocent, but definitely, a prude.

What I meant to communicate was that I couldn't understand the sexual implications of young women showing their legs in bathing suits. Both bathing suits and legs were for swimming, didn't people know that? But my naiveté was real, and apparent, and I liked to think most Hollywood people thought it was, at least, refreshing.

The slant of this publicity seemed to follow me, even when I was put under contract to Universal Studios several years later. A young producer who became a close friend cast me as the lead in his film, *Love, Honor, and Oh, Baby.* He was walking down the street at Universal Studios with a man who was an assistant director. I was walking behind them, just far enough to hear their conversation. They were talking about me.

I heard Don say, to the assistant director, "Well, you know, she is a very nice girl."

And the friend laughed, and said, "I know. I don't like her either."

By that time, I had been immersed in the tale that a girl couldn't get anywhere in Hollywood unless you "slept with" somebody who could get you somewhere. So, I knew very well what the remark was all about, and I thought it was funny, too. Later, Don and I laughed together, and he forgave me for being "nice". So did the assistant director. Don cast me as the lead in the cliffhanger *Sky Raiders*, as well as almost every other film he produced at Universal. Being "nice" was not the worst thing one could be, a little less lofty than "perfect." It was a reputation I could well live with.

⤜⤳ *Chapter Ten* ⤖⤳

SOMEWHERE IN THE BLUR OF DAYS that followed my visit with Gregory La Cava and signing a contract with RKO, I learned that the film I was to be in would be called, indeed, *Fifth Avenue Girl*. Also, to my bewilderment, I learned that there was to be no script! La Cava's idea was that the plot would unfold as the shooting went along, giving the film a lively immediacy. The writer would confer with La Cava at the end of the day to discuss how the story would unfold, and then, Mr. Scott would go home and prepare the script for the following day. The role I was cast in was the daughter of a very wealthy man, played by the excellent character actor Walter Connelly. His wife in the film was gracious Veree Teasdale; their son, Tim Holt, son of the very famous cowboy actor, Jack Holt. This was to be the very first non-western Tim would have been in.

This "no script" and casting against type was a most innovative idea that I believe didn't work out as well as La Cava had hoped. For me, it was both frustrating and bewildering. My idea of "acting" was to become acquainted with the character one was to portray, and internalize it. All my experience in acting had emerged from that idea.

My wardrobe was made by Howard Greer, one of Hollywood's finest wardrobe designers. I was chauffeured to his studio and delivered back to the Studio Club everyday.

The first days of shooting, I learned a lot — how to "hit my marks," how to pretend to start eating the box of chocolates set before me, before "the take". La Cava told me gently that film acting was not at all like The Stage. In films, you didn't project, you forgot the audience and let your personality shine through! Film acting was a matter of personality, and he urged me every day to "just be natural" which was a total enigma to me.

So, day after day, I flounced around in my gorgeous clothes, trying to be "natural" as La Cava insisted I be, with no idea whatsoever of what the "natural" me really was. I'd have found it much easier to be bare-footed, dressed in cut-off overalls, carrying a fishing pole. But I couldn't possibly have suggested that. Not the daughter of a millionaire, a "Fifth Avenue Girl!" So I did the best I could, which really wasn't very good, and thought about what the folks back home would think.

The first day of shooting, I was shown to my dressing room, and there was a bouquet of roses and a portable radio with my name "Kathryn Adams" engraved on it. Portable radios were new in those days.

I hadn't got used to the name the studio gave me, because I couldn't think of a good Minnesota name to replace Hohn, long O. Katherine Anderson had already been taken by a fine stage actress. There already was a Linda Christian. So I accepted their christening without protest.

The next overwhelming surprise came when I walked onto the set from my dressing room and heard the piano playing, loudly, "Minnesota Hats Off To Thee!" and everybody clapped! La Cava had a pianist playing between takes "to keep everyone calm and relaxed," he explained. After that first day, I arrived on the set to the soft strains of "Begin the Beguine," the Mills Brothers, and a bit of soft classical music. La Cava had the pianist drop the loud Minnesota greeting, and when I walked on the set he just called out, "Here comes the Minnesota Bubble!"

I worried a bit about what Ginger Rogers thought about all this attention, but never found out. She was polite, but seemed remote to me.

La Cava gave me very little direction. He was always warm and gracious, suggested that during a lull, when I was not needed for filming, I should ask his chauffeur to drive me down to the beach, miles away, for a swim and basking in the sun. I couldn't possibly have taken him up on this offer. I was embarrassed at the thought! So I stayed on the set and read.

Instead of laughing and enjoying the attention I was getting and saying thank you, I was speechless, wondering what Ginger was thinking. She was in her dressing room and only came out for the takes. She was always courteous to me, but quiet and understandably unenthusiastic about the Minnesota Bubble.

Hugh Beaumont was as puzzled as I about the "just be natural" advice, since his coach, Elias Day, director of the Long Beach Players in Long Beach, California, had advised his actors to study the part deeply and carefully to "get the feel of the part." That made sense to me. But La Cava's way was an unknown. Without a script, how could I study the part? But I bumbled along as best I could and the days dragged by. And the months as March became April and then May.

It was during that first seasonal change that the longing for *home* began to disturb my sleep and flatten my interest in my newly born film career. In California there was so little change in the weather, no noticeable return of migrating birds, the dramatic lengthening of daylight and shortening of dark night. And, as the spring months rolled by, and the days grew longer and the darkness swiftly shorter, the time came when we could start to pack away our winter comforters, release into the warming air our blue jeans and swimming suits and start our longed for yearly trip "Up to the Lake!"

Now, in the same-all-the-time California, I was a working girl. In between takes on the set of *Fifth Avenue Girl*, I sat in my special director's chair without much to do but read, and memories of "Camp Laf–a–Lot" filled my being, almost erasing from my mind the lines I needed to remember from the script given to me that morning.

I longed to be going up to the lake, to listen again to the pine trees sing through the screens of our red tarpaper covered cabin, and the rain drumming on the roof, to feel the caress of dew-drenched grasses beneath my bare feet. I longed to walk into the woods to greet the wildflowers, and sing their names in my made-up melody: pasque flower, columbine, anemone. I longed to search the tree tops for the scarlet tanager, and say "hello" to the returning rose-breasted grosbeak, thanking it for bringing me the message of returning life and beauty as it fluttered into my awareness on wings. Most of all, I longed, once more, to tiptoe into the, clean, clear, nonchlorinated, sky-blue water, pat my tummy, then plunge in; and, feeling the water gliding over me, stretch my arms, kick my legs and *swim*.

I longed to be reunited with my family again, as it was when I was a child — my mother, my father, my brothers. I wanted with all my heart to see the excitement of my cousins, aunts and uncles after a great fishing day, and listen to the laughter when someone told a "dirty" joke, which my father often did. Although many jokes were told in German, which made them seem less bawdy, I was proud of my family's not being pious.

My relationship with my mother was different in the summer, too. After both my brothers had left home to go to college, to go here and there to learn about life, and my father's ministering kept him where ever his pastorate happened to be, Mama and I were often at Camp Laf–a–Lot by ourselves. I enjoyed being with her alone, the nearest neighbor being miles away through the woods. She seemed to fear nothing, not the bats that sometimes whirred above our heads at night and that we caught with a butterfly net and released into the blackness outside, nor the skunk that crawled under the cabin, nor lightning storms that shook the rafters. None of it. I took her courage and spunk for granted and felt safe. When winter came, with school — classmates, popularity and grades, that Summer — Mama was forgotten.

At the lake she chopped wood and cooked on a tiny wood stove with a miniature oven that held only one pie. My father built a small platform for the little stove so she wouldn't have to bend over so far as she fried fish and baked. She often cooked for ten to fourteen people on that tiny bit of cast iron. Though it was difficult in many ways, both my parents enjoyed the primitive life, kerosene lamps, candles, outdoor "biffy" (lots of jokes about that), all of it.

We did some baking together. I carried water in a blue enamel pail from a pump down the hill to the east of the cabin. I spent hours taming chipmunks that would follow the trail of nuts I had placed under the hazelnut bushes leading to me. I would sit motionless for hours it seemed, until finally, joy of joys, one would jump onto my open, nut-filled hands.

I walked barefoot for miles along the sandy beach without passing one cabin or seeing another soul. (I had promised not to go into the water by myself.) One year I found a strange carcass of a fish and ran to my mother with the news. When the neighboring farmer arrived with the milk and the mail for us, he went down to the beach with me to see it and declared it was a lake sturgeon that had once lived in our Lake Pokegama in abundance.

Those days, with my mother alone, I felt brave, strong, adventurous — the half-wild, fearless tomboy I had forgotten for so many years. In those days I entertained thoughts of becoming an explorer someday and going off into unknown wildernesses.

And it was here at Camp Laf–a–Lot that the bond with my father took on another dimension. Mama was the cook, housekeeper and kitchen person. It was my father who took me out onto the water to fish, or into the beautiful, clean blue lake to seine for minnows. He watched me swim. And — he took me into the woods!

When I was a very little girl and Mama and I were expecting him to come from our winter home, I would wait the entire day. Barefoot, as always, "brown as a berry," tousle-haired and dressed in overalls, I would walk along the trail that led through the woods. I put my ear to the ground as I had learned the Indians did, trying to catch the vibrations of the car grinding its way through the woods, hours before the expected time. When he finally arrived, car full of food and "goodies", real life would begin with jellied orange slices, Baby Ruth bars, caramel corn.

In our Northwoods home with father, there were hikes across the meadow to the place where pin cherries and choke cherries grew. He would pick me up in his arms and support me so that I could reach the heavy clusters of red and purple berries hanging above my head. He lifted me out of bed at dawn one summer morning just so I could see the miracle of sunlit dew on the spider webs that wrapped the spruce and balsam trees near the cabin. Millions of diamonds festooned the trees, more glorious than any Christmas tree I could imagine. It was in his arms I saw this wondrous transformation.

He lifted me up in his arms and gently parted the branches of a balsam tree, so that I could see the tiny speckled eggs and later, the baby birds, nestled there. We would tiptoe away before he set me down, to keep from frightening the mother bird. And in the evenings he would hold me on his left arm while he put the index and baby finger of his right hand in his mouth to call the whip-poor-will. We would listen intently for the "Whip-poor-will, whip-poor-will" as the shy evening bird's answer would come closer and closer.

In summer, Father was not the great figure in the frock coat, standing in front of the congregation, tall and angular, waving his Dürer hands and booming out the hymns above all the other voices. This was a warm, intimate, quieter man in an old red sweater, whittling things and weaving baskets from reeds he picked along the shore of the lake, singing in a soft voice with his heavy German accent, "Scheeters ama hummin' on de honeysuckle vine, schleep Kentucky pape" or "In de gloamin', oh my darlin'." This was a man who held me on his lap to read to me, stories, poetry. His lap was longer and more firm than Mama's. Her lap was warm and soft like the comforter I loved to sleep under, but it was short and slippery, and I slid off easily. Father's lap held me secure.

That is what was missing now, far away, in Southern California, in *Hollywood* — being held securely. And it was in those change of season months that my homesickness, my longing for Paradise, mingled with fear of the Great Unknown New Life, had deepened into the overwhelming grief for the father I had lost two far away years ago. Even Hugh Beaumont's fatherly comfort did not assuage my sorrow.

One of those lonely nights a terrifying dream wakened me. Before my dream eyes, Camp Laf–a–Lot and all of Lake Pokegama were being brutally engulfed in an enormous earthquake, and the well-known, beloved place of both solace and delight was covered with lifeless, molten lava.

Chapter Eleven

As may segued into June, I knew it was time for my mother to pack her bags and travel, not "Up to the Lake," but to Hollywood, California, to see her one and only daughter in her new life in the movies. I had such mixed feelings about it. I loved my mother in a way, but she was so Midwestern, so naive, I thought. How could she possibly fit in? And she would meet Hugh Beaumont, far more worldly-wise than any of the men she had ever known. What would she think about him?

But she was coming, no doubt about it, and I prepared for her with both apprehension and a measure of excitement. I found an apartment for us close to Aunt Emmeline and Uncle Jake and awaited her arrival with distinctly mixed feelings.

She arrived about mid-June, travel weary, but triumphant. The first thing she noticed were the oleanders and hibiscus that were in bloom, and she thought they were just beautiful.

From the very first day when I took mother onto the set with me, everyone from La Cava to script girls, cameramen, wardrobe and makeup people, were warm and welcoming, and not one person raised eyebrows at the entry of this little Midwestern minister's wife.

Allan Scott, the writer of *Fifth Avenue Girl*, and his wife invited us to dinner in their beautiful home on Mulholland Drive, overlooking the San Fernando Valley. As we drove up the hills, we both admired the sight of the few lights that twinkled far down in the valley below. The Scotts had invited a former Minnesotan, the fine actor Walter Abel and we shared some Minnesota stories. Mrs. Scott entertained us with a raunchy medieval song, accompanying herself on the guitar. Every verse ended with the chorus, "a funny little dingle-dangle hanging down by his side." Did my mother know what a dingle-dangle was? But she laughed heartily at the end of the song and clapped her hands with the rest of us. Maybe there was a German version of dingle-dangle that my father may have sung, back home.

"That was a lovely evening," Mama said as we drive down from the Hollywood Hills to The Valley below. Hollywood and Mother had passed the first test, and I smiled to myself as I drove home to my apartment.

Then came the strangest event of all that first summer in Hollywood with my mother. And it came on a Sunday afternoon.

The Sundays of my childhood and adolescence were the crown of the week. No Day of Rest for my parents. It was Sunday School, church and, very often, company after church. My father was one of those ministers who did not like to retreat into solitude after church. The glow of performance, of having given it his all, was still upon him. He needed to talk, to be engaged in an informal way with his parishioners. Often he would spot newcomers in the congregation and invite them to Sunday dinner after the service.

My mother accepted this ritual and seemed to enjoy it as much as my father. Saturday baking prepared her for it. Sunday before Sunday School the table was set. My job.

"How many?" I would ask.

"Oh, set a few extra," my mother would answer. "I don't know how many your father will invite. We can always squeeze in a few more."

Potatoes were peeled, covered with water, ready to boil, chicken in the oven, timed to reach doneness just when church was out. Vegetables were cleaned, ready to steam, molded salad in the fridge, and angel food cake, which both my mother and father often baked, in its place of honor on our glass cake plate.

A leisurely, comfortable afternoon followed the meal, chess or checkers for the men, chitchat for the women, Rook or Hearts if there were more than two guests. Most card games were allowed even on Sunday in our liberal household (with the exception of bridge — or poker, of course.) Going to movies on Sundays was forbidden, even though Sunday matinees were cheaper. My mother even did handwork on Sundays, but never sat at the sewing machine.

As a child, and even as I became a teenager, I never questioned the idiosyncratic nature of these permissions and limits on Sunday behaviors. I don't remember the logic ever being explained to me. I don't know how I learned the regulations, and I never rebelled against them. I was proud of our modernism.

Sundays in Hollywood seemed like another matter entirely to those of us so far from the scene. Did anyone of the film crowd ever go to church? In those days that seemed like uncharacteristic behavior. Interest in religion from esoteric to charismatic to fundamental was not publicized as part of the Hollywood scene.

So what did movie people do on Sundays, we wondered. Golf? Polo? Horse races, all manner of activities not really sinful, but time-wasting, and expensive? But movie stars were like many ministers, I discovered, and did not like to twinkle alone. And so, Sunday afternoons many gathered round their swimming pools, the beach, patios, for cocktails, barbecues, the latest Hollywood gossip and shop talk.

When La Cava hospitably invited me to his beautiful beach house at Malibu La Costa (which he wryly named "La Costa Plenta") he thoughtfully included my mother. I was pleased. I was terrified. Now my mother would see, for the first time, how Hollywood people, off work, really lived. Now she would see liquor flow freely, hear slurred speech and raucous laughter, experience a kind of inebriated conviviality.

I had already experienced a good bit of this. My first Christmas away from home, La Cava had invited me, and Hugh also, to his home in Beverly Hills and I watched in stupefied wonder as the guests sat around the table and threw cheese balls at the chandeliers, singing "Oh, Come All Ye Faithful" in gleeful, drunken, off-key tones. My homesickness and sadness was so deep, I had to leave the party early before anyone passed out. La Cava thoughtfully called me the following day and apologized.

My mother had never experienced this kind of party in all her life, and as Sunday grew closer I was beginning to feel protective, embarrassed and extremely ill at ease. (Why did I think I was so much more sophisticated and adaptable than my mother after only six months in Hollywood?)

The Sunday arrived. Mama dolled up in her Sunday best for the big day. I discouraged a hat. This was California, I said. This was a beach party. I helped her put on more lipstick than she was used to wearing and we were finally ready to go out the door. At the last moment, however, my mother, succumbing to years of habit, picked up the tapestry bag that held her handwork and said, "I think I'll take my crocheting."

"Mother!" I answered, appalled at a parent's behavior as only a teenager can be.

"Well, she said, confident and contained, "I'll only take it out if there's nothing else to do. I won't know anybody, so rather than sit with my hands folded, I'll do some handwork."

So off we sped in my little brown second-hand Plymouth coupe to Malibu beach to a Sunday afternoon Hollywood cocktail party, all dressed up, well made up, my swim suit in a beach bag and my happy Midwestern minister's wife mother and her ubiquitous bag of crocheting.

When we reached La Cava's beach house, we were warmly welcomed as though we were honored guests. After all, we were La Cava's young protégé and her mother from Minny-so-ta. We were immediately offered a drink. Our considerate host turned to the eldest first. "Mrs. Hohn, may I serve you a drink? What would you like?"

"Oh," said my mother, casually, innocently, "how nice. Well, actually. A glass of root beer would be very nice."

No one gasped, but La Cava quietly sent his chauffeur to the nearest Sunday-open market for a case of root beer.

I had warned my mother I might accept a glass of sparkling burgundy, the only alcoholic beverage I had learned to swallow and like. La Cava knew I favored this sparkling wine and told me he had case on hand for me. After all, it wouldn't be polite not to appreciate his thoughtfulness and accept his offer. Sparkling burgundy sounded very special and whatever it was, it didn't really seem like liquor. And my father had been known to relish wine, and the man who made the wine for Catholic communion in his last parish in Crookston, Minnesota, had slipped him a bottle now and then. Not yet blessed, of course. A glass of wine occasionally certainly wouldn't start a decline down the Primrose Path, now, would it?

After being introduced all around, La Cava took my mother by the arm and gallantly escorted her to a gentleman sitting straight-backed on a chair, hands folded protectively over the head of a cane propped between his knees.

"This, Mrs. Hohn, is my friend, Mr. W. C. Fields. Bill, this is my protégé's mother, Mrs. Hohn from "Minny-so-ta.""

This was an electric moment. My minister's wife mother and W. C. Fields, one of the greatest comedians of all time, perhaps the most foul-mouthed, al-coholic actor in all of Hollywood, meeting one another. Fields happened to be one of the very few actors my mother knew anything about. She had seen him in *My Little Chickadee* with Mae West and thought he was the funniest man she could imagine. And one night she dreamed she had married him! "Why, Katya," she had said with an embarrassed giggle, "why in the world would I dream a thing like that?"

Why, indeed, I had thought, back then dismissing her dream and her puzzle-ment. On this unimagined occasion, Mr. Fields raised one hand from the tip of his cane, gesturing toward the empty chair beside him, and my mother sat down. My heart stopped.

La Cava took my arm and escorted me around the room, introducing me to his other guests, so I had to turn my head now and then to keep track of my mother. I could not see her face, but I caught her nodding in a small queenly way and then heard them both chuckle.

I was nervous the entire afternoon. Understandably. I went for a swim, learn-ing, with a few tumbles, how to catch the cresting wave and ride home with it.

I drank a sparkling burgundy or two, nibbled appetizers, chatted with some of the other guests about Minny-so-ta, what brought me to Hollywood, how I liked acting in the movies. And in between, I watched my mother.

I needn't have worried. Unbelievably, she and Mr. Fields seemed to be having a wonderful time. Neither of them moved an inch the entire afternoon. Mr. Fields just sat. My mother sat and crocheted.

I knew Field's reputation as Hollywood's greatest lush. Maybe this afternoon, he was too drunk to stand. I had heard stories that his valet was supposed to keep an eye on him, to watch over him to hold down his drinking. But, the story goes, he found ingenious ways to outwit his guardian. It was told that he had a special cane made, with a hollow top that would hold a shot or two of whiskey when needed and no one was looking.

But, this afternoon, he stayed seated, seemingly sober, focused on my mother. One time I heard him laugh aloud and say, in his famous gravely voice, "Well, little lady, that's just great!"

I don't remember one thing about the goodbyes. I only remember the ride home, my mother, tapestry bag intact on her lap, spilling over with wonder about her Sunday afternoon with Mr. W. C. Fields.

"Why, Kathy," she said with a little giggle. "Can you believe it? W. C. Fields, the man I dreamed I married. And we talked the entire afternoon. He is the nicest man! I told him all about the Orphan's Home, Tarzan and the boys, and the girls I left behind. And he told me all about his childhood. So sad. He ran away from home to join the circus when he was just a little boy. And he talked about how he got started drinking. And the evils of alcohol. He was so nice. I just can't get over it!"

We were both silent then, I with relief; my mother, I guessed, still filled with wonder over the strange encounter with Mr. W. C. Fields of Hollywood, and the unimaginable turn her life was taking.

After the long shared silence, my mother gave her tapestry bag a firm pat, a period to this unlikely episode.

"And guess what, Katya," my mother announced brightly, "I got six medallions crocheted!"

Chapter Twelve

WAS THIS THE EXPERIENCE THAT BEGAN THE LONG JOURNEY of seeing and experiencing my mother in a new light, coming "home" after a long absence as Thomas Wolfe wrote, and "seeing the place for the first time?" Was my ordinary mother actually extraordinary in her own way? Now, far from home in Hollywood, forgotten mother-daughter experiences emerged. I began to look at my mother with freshly opened eyes.

My childhood and adolescent memories were of a plump Mama who fussed at me continually, it seemed. When I thought of her back then, I was reminded of a scolding chipmunk, chattering away, tail twitching constantly, all about little everyday things, like picking up my toys and washing my hands before supper. So very different from the tall, grave, but warm and "holy" man I knew as my father.

But now, in this totally new setting, flashbacks of my earliest years unreeled in my mind, one after the other. There was not only the memory of my disaster on the top of my father's desk, and Mama's rescuing me and mending the unholy hole in my dress; but vivid close-ups of her face emerged in my inward vision lustily singing the alto part in Handel's Messiah, "For the Lord God Omnipotent reigneth! Alleluia!" My mother, not just my father, loved music. I could not have been more than five years old when she made the long ride with me in the caboose of the train that ran from New Ulm to Minneapolis just to hear the immortal Fritz Kreisler play his violin.

And it was she who most often listened to my bedtime prayers.

Then came the memory of the infamous "No Birthday Party" and my mother's redemption of a near disaster. I have written a story about this event for my grandchildren some time ago. I am drawing from that story now as I retell it, and hopefully with more insight.

This infamous party took place in Prospect Park in Minneapolis after our move back to Minnesota from Central Wesleyan Orphans Asylum in Missouri.

This party had its beginning before our move, I believe. One day, during our last days at the orphanage, I had complained to my father, with heartfelt tears, that he spent much more time with the orphans than he did with me — took them on trips, played ball with the boys when he got home, and had their

66

pictures taken with him holding armloads of orphans. And they called him "Daddy Hohn". I hardly ever saw him, I sobbed. He was my daddy, so why didn't I get to be with him?

My father listened patiently, then took me on his lap and carefully explained the plight of the orphans, many of whom had never known a parent, especially a father, who actually may have abandoned them. He explained that he took the orphans on trips, because their presence and their singing helped him raise money to make the orphanage an even better place. And the boys needed to be with a grown man, someone they could look up to, and love.

"I was hoping and praying, my dear daughter, that you would have it in your heart to understand and be generous, knowing their pain," he said, a sad look on his face. He hugged me then and told me he loved me more than anything in the world and was sorry he had caused me hurt.

But I was not comforted. I slid down off his lap and carried my sorrow and my shame to bed with me.

After that he did try to spend more time with me, but it was very little. I tried with all my might to "understand" as I saw him out in the field playing ball with the boys. Guilty feelings stayed with me. I understood that it was not quite fair and right, somehow, that I was overprivileged by having a father who loved me, when many children did not know their father even existed.

Not many months after that, my father resigned from his position as executive director of the orphanage. He put in a request to the Methodist bishop to find him a parish in Minnesota, and very shortly was assigned to the Prospect Park Methodist Church in Minneapolis. We said many tearful goodbyes and we moved.

After our arrival and we had settled in, parishioners would often ask why we left the orphanage. And both my parents would respond, "Because of our beloved only daughter's health."

And it was probably true. Before we left Missouri, I had been steadily losing weight, was "skinny as a rail", every day ran a bit of a fever, and became listless about my dearly loved school work.

One day, not long after our arrival in Minnesota, my mother was cleaning with her German housewifely vigor and my father and I were in the living room helping her dust. Mama was reaching down into the crevasses of our overstuffed chair with the vacuum cleaner attachment when the rattle of paper stopped her. She reached down to pull it out. There it was, a crumpled note, and on it, this inscription, which she read aloud:

Dear Mama Hohn,

By the time you find this note, you will be long gone and far away. But we want you to know that no matter how far away you are, we will never forget you, how kind and loving you were, how much you taught us. We will love you forever.

Your Orphan Girls

The note was signed with the signature of each of her High School helpers.

My mother pulled the crumpled paper to her heart and burst into sobs. Her tears came from a deep place within her, I knew. "Oh those dear girls," she sobbed, "I do so wonder where they are and how they are. How could I have left them?"

But she had, on the advice of Father Giesler, who believed it was best for my parents not to keep in touch with the children in order for them to make the adjustment more quickly.

I left my father to comfort Mama, walked upstairs to my bedroom and shut the door. How could my selfishness and my "poor health" cause so much suffering? I fell onto my bed and let my own tears flow.

Shortly after our arrival in our new home, I had been taken to a doctor and given X-Rays; and it was discovered I did, indeed, have spots on my lungs as well as a mild, but positive reaction to the tuberculin test. For this reason the doctors advised my parents to send me to a "fresh-air" school, which happened to be Lymanhurst, at Chicago and Eighteenth Street in Minneapolis. I went there every day and came home on the street car with tokens provided by the school. There, we children were on a relaxed academic schedule, had sun lamp treatments, special exercises, and we were treated with both warmth and respect. Our tuberculin tests were administered regularly.

But even though Lymanhurst was a fine experience for me, in many ways, it delayed my becoming acquainted with the children in the Sydney Pratt Public Elementary School across the street from the parsonage.

Each day, coming home from Lymanhurst on the street car, I came into an empty house. Mama was gone, to church meetings, no doubt; and now that Father's study was in the church, he was gone, too. My oldest brother, Roland, was attending the University of Minnesota graduate school; and Win, busy being a popular teenager, never seemed to be at home.

Every day, after school, I would go to my room, shut the door, and let the loneliness flood my being. I missed the orphans, missed a few close friends

I had made at Lymanhurst. I didn't really know anyone in my classroom at Sydney Pratt and had no idea how to begin to make friends. No one seemed to reach out to me. Were they afraid they would catch T.B.? I would not have been released from Lymanhurst, if I had been contagious. But maybe they didn't know that.

Alone in the house and in my room, I wrapped my arm in a dish towel sling to handicap myself for being unhealthy, a left-handed, overprivileged and selfish girl. I forced myself to study the subjects I was poorest at — arithmetic and spelling.

Maybe it was while I was trying to remember how to spell "festival" that the idea came to me! A party! That was it! I'd have a party and invite a few of the girls in my class, and we'd have fun and get to know each other!

I asked my mother if I couldn't please have a party and she crisply said no, not now, she was too busy. My entreaties, my tears, were of no use. So, in desperation, I invited six girls to my house for a party, this coming Saturday at two o'clock!

Saturday came, and I had not said one word to my mother that I had asked six girls over this very afternoon!

That morning I dusted, I ran the carpet sweeper, put the living room in order, and accepted my mother's praise for being such a good helper. As Gramma's clock ticked toward two o'clock, I called out, "Mama, think I'll wash up and put on some clean clothes," and ran upstairs.

I quickly washed my face and under my arms as my mother had taught me, and put on my Sunday best dress.

Ting–Ting. Two o'clock! Gramma's clock was never too fast or too slow. Mama wound it every day.

The door bell rang. I ran downstairs to open the door before my mother could get there. There stood three girls all dressed up in their Sunday best. Very shortly, the door bell rang again. This time my mother beat me to the door, opened it, and exclaimed, "Oh my, how pretty!"

She invited my guests into the living room, waved her hand slightly, saying "Have a good time" and disappeared into the kitchen.

I did the best I could to entertain my hopefully newfound friends. I had collected all my games, tiddlywinks, Parcheesi, both of which I had stashed in my closet the day before. I had wrapped my unopened colored pencils and jigsaw puzzle for prizes for the game winners. All seven of us were having such a good time, I almost forgot about my mother.

Just when it seemed as though the time had come to say good-bye, Mama came into the living room. In her hand she carried a tray of frosted cup cakes with a candle on each.

"Girls," said my mother, sweet as could be. "Our Katya has a birthday in July, when we are gone Up North, so we can't have a party for her then. So this is her celebration, her 'No Birthday Party'. Come into the dining room. I have some whipped Jello for you to go with your cup cakes. I have strawberry and cherry. You can choose."

The table had been beautifully set with our best china, and candles. She even had our special nut cups filled with chocolate kisses and jelly beans.

The girls seemed to have a lovely time. And I did start to make friends.

When my father came home and saw the table and the crumbs, he said, "Well, what have we here?"

And my mother answered sweetly, "Well, Katya and I had a little surprise party, a 'No Birthday Party'."

That's all she said. But that night she tucked me in bed for the first time in weeks and kissed my forehead. "Katya, I'm sorry. I've been so busy. I didn't realize how much you needed a party."

I couldn't think of anything to say. Not even, "Thank you." I was numb with gratitude. I put my arms around my mother and hugged her tight. When she turned out my light and left the room, I breathed, "Now I lay me down to sleep — and dear God, thank you for my mother."

How could I, in my adolescent years, have so completely forgotten this day and this mother?

⟨⟩ *Chapter Thirteen* ⟨⟩

BUT NOW, MANY LONG YEARS LATER, this almost forgotten mother was sitting by my side as we rode silently back into the San Fernando Valley from the beach in Malibu, California. I knew the mother whose life work was kitchen, garden and handwork. I knew well the busy mother bustling about our home, the Methodist parsonage, wherever it was, keeping it supremely clean; and when she sat to "rest" picking up her handwork, embroidering dish towels and pillow cases in July for Christmas gifts in December.

This very day that forever busy mother couldn't just sit. Even in the presence of a famous human being, Mr. W. C. Fields, she had to be doing something other than sitting with her hands folded in her lap. She listened, she crocheted, and yes, she talked! This was the mother I had let slip into unawareness. This was a story-telling mother.

Now in the silence of our journey along the Malibu Highway and through the hills toward The Valley, images of my mother telling her stories filled my mind. I saw her repeating the dramatic events of our lives to friends, family, dinner guests, church women's gatherings. I realized in those moments for the first time in my life, my mother was a wonderful storyteller, and she had wonderful stories to tell. Telling those stories again and again, she became, without knowing it, the family historian.

And the story she told this day apparently touched something in the man she told it to. Maybe he was putting her on. Maybe his offbeat sense of humor caused him to humor her. Something in me doubted that. In that moment, I remembered his hearty laugh, his voice ringing out above the chatter. Had Mr. W. C. Fields picked up something genuine in my mother that he spontaneously responded to?

The story is one that I had heard so often, I had memorized it, and even written about in my second published book *Wild Orphan*. In that story my father and mother are portrayed as Onkel and Tante and, I believe, are quite accurate presentations.

My father had left his ministry in New Ulm, Minnesota, to take the job raising money for the Central Wesleyan Orphans Asylum in Missouri. He had admired a Jewish orphanage that built separate cottages housing ten to twelve children, each cottage to have two adults who would watch over and care for them, as much like caring parents as possible.

When there was enough money to complete the second cottage at Central Wesleyan, my father could find no one to be housemother to the forty (not ten to twelve!) children that were to be housed there. This arrangement was to be a temporary one, until enough money could be raised to build more cottages.

After watching my father agonize over that dilemma, my mother finally agreed to take on the job, and the only help she had was from four or five high school girls who had been assigned to her cottage. My mother loved those children, ages six to sixteen. She fed, listened to them complain, and watched over them as though they were her own.

My father was gone a lot, and nothing had been agreed upon as far as the disciplining of the children was concerned. That issue was the occasion for the bubbling over of the dislike my mother felt for the superintendent, Father Giesler. He was a gruff, irritable man who didn't really like or understand children. He beat them so severely when they broke a rule that their backs broke open and bled, and they had to lie on their stomachs for many days while their backs healed.

One day my mother "bearded the old lion in his den" to put it in her own words. The occasion arose when three of "her little boys" got into trouble. The orphanage was a farm and pigs were raised, as well as some cows and a few horses. The children loved to climb the apple trees that hung over the pig pen, pick the green apples and throw them down for the pigs to gobble up, and then watch the poor pigs squeal and roll around in the mud from the tummy aches they got.

This unforgettable day, three of mother's little boys got caught doing just that, and some of the older boys ran to Father Giesler, who marched out to the pig pen, caught the boys in the act, ordered them down from the tree, and hauled them to the Big House, where most of the children were housed.

In remembering my mother telling this story to Mr. Fields, I can just imagine her stopping her furious crocheting at this point, laying it in her lap, and with a little laugh, look at the great man before she went on. This is her story, so it must be told in her own words:

You know, Mr. Fields, the wonderful little boys I knew at the orphanage must have been a lot like you. They were lively and daring, but warm and funny. Oh, I knew they had to be disciplined. But I had my own way of doing it. My husband would have talked to them, reasoned with them. I would give them something hard to do around the cottage and put them to bed without their supper. A glass of milk, maybe. No dessert.

When my husband saw the boys the time they had been beaten for swimming in their birthday suits in the little pool out in the woods and Father Giesler had beaten them, Christian right away called the trustees to come from St. Louis and see the boys lying on their stomachs, bleeding lacerations on their backs. They came and saw and went home, still not decided on how to deal with the problem.

Well, this wasn't going to happen to my boys ever, I'll tell you! When my littlest boys had been tattled on and taken directly to Father Giesler's office, without even talking to me, I was so mad! No one was going to beat my boys like that. Something stiffened me up inside. It must have been what my husband would call righteous indignation, because without even thinking about it, I marched right over to the Big House.

The first thing I saw when I walked in that door, was three of my boys huddled together, sort of scrunched over, under the stairwell outside Giesler's office.

"It's all right, Henry, Fritz, Tarzan. I'm here to take you home."

Those boys were wide-eyed and shaking, so I could hardly wait to get to Father Giesler. I walked right up to his door and knocked. But when he said, 'who is it?' I shook inside and my heart was pounding so hard I could hear it. But I went right on.

"It's me, Anna Hohn. I need to talk to you!"

"Just a minute. I'm on the phone!" His gruff voice scared me. My heart was beating so fast you'd think I'd have a heart attack.

Where did I get the courage to practically shout back, "You can hang up and call later. I need to talk to you now! It's important."

In a minute he came to the door, ushered me into his office and pointed to a chair. But I wasn't going to sit down. No, siree! I waited for him to sit and then I faced him and practically shouted, "What are you doing with my boys?"

He tried to scowl me down, but I wasn't going to have it. Not this time. I plowed right on, "I understood that the last time you and my husband talked, I was to do the disciplining when Christian was away."

"Well," he hemmed and hawed, "we didn't agree altogether. You were to discipline for the things inside the cottage. For things on the farm —."

I didn't even let him finish. I just went right on, getting madder all the time. "You mean to tell me you intend to beat those little boys for throwing green apples to the pigs, beat them 'til they bleed?"

The old geezer just leaned back in his chair and looked at me as though I was a child and he said, can you imagine, "Well, these orphans need strong discipline. That's all they understand. It's the only way they will remember."

I must have been really fired up. I can't believe what I really did and said, but the next thing you know I was pointing my finger out the window and saying, "Father Giesler, you have a beautiful little grand-daughter that lives right there, across the street from this orphanage. Would you beat her like that if she disobeyed?'"

He turned around and looked daggers at me. I thought my heart would stop.

"Anna, that's entirely different and you know it. My granddaughter is a legitimate child. Born in wedlock to church-going parents. These — these orphans are bastards, born in sin. That tendency is bred into them by their parents and it has to be beaten out of them. It's our Christian duty. It's the only way they can learn."

"Well, it's not my idea of our Christian duty," I heard myself say. "Our Christian duty is to suffer the little children to come unto me. How can they be blamed for the mistakes of their parents. My Christian duty is to take these children by the hand and take them *home* and put them to bed without any supper. Well, milk, maybe."

I didn't give him a single minute to say another thing. I just marched right out of his office and turned to the children huddled under the stairwell.

"'Come on, boys,' I said, "We're going home." And I took Tarzan's hand and led him out ot there.

Those frightened little boys didn't say a word. They just followed me like little puppies. As soon as we got out of the Big House, Tarzan grabbed my chubby arm right above my elbow, and squeezed so hard it hurt like the dickens. But I just let him hang on, and Henry and Fritz just trotted along on the other side, close to me. On our way to our cottage, some older boys who were raking in the field beside us called out, "Hey, Tarzan, didja get beat up?"

Tarzan squeezed my arm even tighter, calling back, "No, but we woulda had, if it hadn't been for Mama Hohn!"

Did my mother stop at this point, chuckling again, pat the knee of the great Mr. W. C. Fields, punctuating her story with one last remark? "That made everything I'd been through worth the thumping of my heart. And the black and blue marks on my arm from Tarzan's squeezing fingers were totally worth the pain, you better believe me!"

That must have been the point when I heard Mr. W. C. Fields laugh out loud and say, "Well, little lady, that's just great!"

This was and is a wonderful story and as I remembered it this Sunday afternoon, I wished she could have stayed with Mr. Fields and told him another of her oft-repeated stories, the one I love the most:

It was Wednesday evening, prayer meeting night down in New Ulm, and my husband and I had spent the entire day making sausages. Some farmer had given us half a pig for his pledge to the church and we had butchered it in the kitchen. The sausages were the last thing we had to do. When we finally finished, my husband went upstairs to change his clothes for Wednesday evening prayer meeting. When he came back down all clean and dressed in his frock coat for church, his Bible and hymnal tucked under his arm, he stopped long enough to hug me again saying, "Danke, mein Anna" and started out the back door. When he passed the sausages hanging so neatly on the broom handle, the tail of his frock coat caught on the edge of the handle! And the whole thing crashed to the floor, breaking the sausage casings so that sausage scattered all over the floor. I gasped. Christian said absolutely nothing, not one word. He just stood there looking at the awful mess. Then, he tucked his hymnal and Bible more closely under his arm and went out the back door and on to the prayer meeting in the church next door. I stayed behind, still in my dirty house dress, got down on my hands and knees and cleaned up the mess.

If my mother had had time to tell this story to W. C. Fields, I can just picture her leaning close to him, and with a twinkle in her eyes and a conspiratorial chuckle saying, "Now, Mr. Fields, who do you think was the better Christian?"

Chapter Fourteen

MANY OTHER DELIGHTFUL THINGS happened to my mother and me during those early days of my film career. She showed none of the behavior of the typical stage mother. She asked no questions. She didn't even try to understand the complexities of the film industry. She assumed, I'm guessing, that I understood all about it, which I certainly didn't; but she seemed to accept all that was transpiring in my new life.

She was invited to dinner and cocktail parties with me and to the final bash at the finishing of *Fifth Avenue Girl*. That huge, elaborate party was held on the set, which was, by the way, the same Fifth Avenue mansion as in *Citizen Kane*, grand stairway and all.

While most of the cast and crew and friends of cast and crew were dancing, or milling about eating, drinking, talking and generally making merry, my mother sat on the side against the wall, engaged in lively conversation with character actors who told her fascinating tales of their childhoods and careers in Austria, Russia, England. I can imagine my mother sharing her tales of the Orphan's Home and her childhood on the plains of Nebraska as a German-from-Russia immigrant, teased for her clothes, her accent, and being born in a sod house. And about her own mother, who had come from a wealthy family of textile manufacturers in Russia. She may even have shared her tale of her days helping her butcher father, who drank too much. Together, my mother and her father had butchered pigs, and even, one time, a cow! Mama was an excellent listener and, of course a wonderful story teller herself, punctuating her own stories with her hearty laugh.

Although at first I had been embarrassed by her Midwestern naïveté, I soon learned she was heartily enjoyed for her genuineness and warmth. My mother was finding a comfortable and more than satisfying place in her starlet daughter's life. She learned to leave her crocheting at home. Now, more than ever before, she was fulfilling her life through me.

Then, another blow to the comfortable integrity of our mother-daughter relationship happened, a deeper and more lasting one.

As the days flowed by, I became less and less interested in either my film career or going back to school. I had been so busy trying not to "go Hollywood" that I wasn't going anywhere at all. Two magnetisms lured me further and further from my film career possibilities. One was the expectations and lofty dreams of my father for me. (Would a film career present an opportunity for me to become a "benefit to mankind"?)

The other was becoming just as compelling. I was becoming more and more engrossed in a relationship with Hugh Beaumont.

Hugh fascinated me, and perplexed my mother. She worried because he was so much older than I, and so much more worldly-wise. I knew a different Hugh, one I got to know gradually on trips to Long Beach, which we had shared every Sunday before my mother came to Hollywood. Hugh's mother and young teenaged sister lived there, as did an old uncle of mine, a penniless brother of my mother's. I was the one who had a car, and when I heard Hugh visited his mother and sister on the street car every Sunday, I invited him to go along with me while I visited Uncle Alex.

On the trips through the barren landscape of oil fields on the way to and from Long Beach, we began to share a lot about our lives before Hollywood. And best of all, without a radio in the car, we filled the rumbly little coupe with music of our own making. I learned Hugh had an exceptionally fine bass-baritone voice and I could harmonize by ear. Hugh, of course, did not know Bach or Bortniansky or Schumann, but we both knew some lovely tunes of the day: "Night and Day", "Blue Moon", and our favorite, "Moonlight Madonna".

The music brought us close in a very different and endearing way. I couldn't help but praise Hugh for his beautiful voice and asked him one day if he had ever thought of taking voice lessons.

Hugh responded with a chuckle much like my mother's.

"Well," he said, "my mother always wanted me to take voice lessons, but I resisted firmly. Voice lessons? Ridiculous. I was a football player. No sissy voice lessons for me. But she kept insisting and finally made an appointment with a highly recommended voice teacher and paid for her in advance. For how many lessons, I never knew. I went on the appointed day and was greeted at the door with a hugely proportioned matron. The first thing she asked me to do, when I'd taken off my football jacket, was to stand behind her and put my arms around her so I could feel how she breathed — diaphragmatically, she said. Well, that was a most uncomfortable task. I did as I was told and put my quarterback arms around her. They barely made it but, yes, indeed, I could feel her breathe. Awful as that experience was, the worst was yet to come. The first sheet of music she gave me to sing was, 'Would God I Were a Tender Apple Blossom'. I left and never went back."

With this confession of Hugh's, we both laughed so hard, tears trickled down both our cheeks. I said nothing, but thought what a loss for the film industry, that Beaumont Bass-Baritone voice. Maybe not John Raitt or Howard Keel, but beautiful, indeed.

This was a Hugh my mother did not experience for a long, long time. She wooed him with her remarkable cooking and he gained ten pounds. He responded with praise and finally hugs, and as the days went by I could see those two grew to tolerate, then respect and, finally, genuinely care about one another.

It was during those round trips to Long Beach that we began to share with one another memories of our early lives that neither of us had done since arriving in Hollywood. I feel sure I told him about my father's illness and death, the days, nights, years of incredible suffering; but I did not shed a tear when relating the story to him. I held on tightly to my rational persona. There were many other stories I longed to share, and I quickly felt much more relaxed about some of the most intimate memories of my early life.

There had been much discussion lately about whether or not Mother should have her hair cut, which Hugh had chuckled about. I wanted very much to tell him my feelings about my mother's hair, which, I realize now, had symbolic meaning for me. I wanted him to get to know my mother in a deeper way than their superficial exchanges provided. And I was beginning to want him to become acquainted with the real, not just the reel, ME. So, one evening, after we had returned from our Long Beach trip, I plunged in with a tale from my early years:

Well, Hugh, the night I want to tell you about, it was snowing — one of those soft-flaked, easy snows that silences the world. I was walking softly, too, on my way to the hospital, this time to see my mother who was recovering from a severe gall bladder attack. We had enjoyed a respite from illness after my father's surgery, but now it was my mother who had been besieged with pain.

The day before, my father had called me into his study and seated himself heavily in his swivel chair. He folded his long, tapering fingers and placed them on his knee. What he was about to say was serious, I knew.

"Dear Heart, Mama is very ill. You know that, don't you?"

I nodded, my heart thumping.

"She may have to have her gall bladder removed. We don't know yet. They have asked me at the hospital if they could cut her hair. What do you think?"

Cut her hair! The very thought was appalling. I was too stunned to answer, which was answer enough for my father.

"No — no," he said, pushing himself up from his chair, steadying himself with the cane he now had to use after the surgery had nicked the nerve in his right leg.

"No, we don't need to do that yet. She wouldn't want it, and neither would you, I can see. Neither would I," he added decisively.

My father put his arm around me and gave me a reassuring squeeze. When he looked down at me, I saw tears in his eyes. He released me, took off his glasses, wiped them, and finished the conversation, as he often did, by blowing his great nose that dripped when he cried.

"Well," he said, satisfied that "we" had made the right decision, "That's that! We'll just watch and pray for her speedy recovery." And he dismissed me with a pat on the head, reducing me for the moment to my child status.

In my bed that night, as I lay sleepless, I thought about the childhood nightmare, in which I saw my mother in a barber chair getting her hair cut and my father standing beside her, doing nothing to prevent this catastrophe. Samson and Delilah, the story in the Bible, came vividly to mind. Delilah cut Samson's hair and he lost his strength. Now it was the other way around. Was there something about the way my father, or most men of the era, thought of women that robbed them of their feminine strength? This was 1939, remember, and I was a preschool child when I had that dream.

When I woke that morning, I pictured my mother in the hospital, her hair unbraided, spread out vibrantly against the white pillow. I could not imagine my mother seriously ill, much less with short hair. Everyone must be exaggerating her illness. But I tossed and turned, clinging to optimism, feeling a strange, swollen sensation down in my lower body.

The next morning, shivering in the winter-cold bathroom, I took off my pajamas and noticed there in the crotch, a reddish brown color. Not much, just a faint touch of color. I was thirteen. It was time. Other girls had started already and I was patiently waiting my time.

My mother had prepared me well, unlike her mother, who had told her nothing whatsoever.

"On my way home from school," my mother had told me in her story-telling way, "I started bleeding like a stabbed pig and I was terrified and cried myself to sleep that night and put a piece of an old, torn cotton flannel sheet between my legs to stop the bleeding. I thought it was because of something I had done to myself down there, you know, but I finally told sister Katherine and she told me I had started young and then she told me all about it. She called it 'the curse', and she told me all women had it and it would happen every month from now on."

And now my time had come, and I was quietly, inwardly joyous. I had to tell my mother, as soon as possible. Now we would share the secret world of women and smile together at the wonder of this great mystery, beyond the experience and comprehension of men.

At breakfast Father told me with a lilt in his voice that he'd had a call from the hospital and was told Mama had taken a turn for the better. Surgery would not be necessary. She would just have to restrict her diet, cut down on butter and cream. I could see her that very day. This very evening. Now, indeed, my cup did run over.

I felt anointed, not cursed, as I walked the few miles through the snow to the hospital in the early, wintry dusk. Every step I took was part of a sacred ritual. I knew that truth, even though I could not have named it at the time. The long walk through the snow was an enactment of a sacred rite of passage, and I could hardly wait to to reach my mother to tell her the wondrous thing that my body had accomplished while she lay so sick. I needed her benediction, her confirmation of this threshold of initiation, for which she had prepared me so well.

When I arrived at the hospital, my feet were tingling from the cold, and I was very tired. But a sense of peace and well-being eased my fatigue. A sweet longing filled my body, too, a sensation I was later to call my sad–happy feeling.

When I entered the room, Mama was sitting up in bed, tasting food for the first time in days. The room was warm. Mama looked pale, but radiant.

I couldn't keep the news of my triumph to myself another moment.

"Mother," I said, as soon as I'd kissed her soft cheek. "I think I've started my periods. Not much, but something!"

Mama looked at me with love and pride.

After a time of simply gazing at me, she said, very quietly, "My little daughter. Grown-up, now. Grown-up already in so many ways. Now, you are all grown-up. How wonderful."

She held out her arms to me and we embraced, two women, healthy, together, and blessed.

When I finished my story, Hugh gathered me in his arms. I put my head on his shoulder — and the tears flowed. I knew then that we were headed down a path from which there was no easy return.

Chapter Fifteen

IT SEEMS STRANGE NOW, but I'm unclear just how Hugh's and my decision to marry came about. I know we each had reservations. Hugh felt he could not support a wife and possibly children, which he knew I wanted very much. He already had a mother and a young sister to take care of. I was somewhat concerned about the difference in our ages, wondering if I was too dependent on him to teach me the ways of the world. My mother was not much help in that respect. I came to depend on Hugh to guide me. And there was no doubt we both respected and enjoyed one another.

After *Fifth Avenue Girl*, RKO cast me in bit parts in a number of films, their rationale being that this would give me experience. This way of treating me was much against La Cava's approval. He predicted that I would get lost in that insignificant world. And he was right. But La Cava was a free lance director, and after the filming of *Fifth Avenue Girl* he left RKO for Metro–Goldwyn –Mayer, where he tried to sell me as the lead in some big film. But the studio insisted he use one of their own upcoming starlets, whose "boobs" were more significant than mine. La Cava was miserable with her. "She was dumb," he said, "and chewed gum the entire time between takes, even when she was talking to me."

We kept in touch until his untimely death, but I never made another film with him.

However, while still under contract to RKO I did a bit in a film, *That's Right, You're Wrong*, starring Kay Kaiser, the very popular band leader and radio star. The director was Dave Butler, who had directed a number of Bing Crosby and Bob Hope films. He was a large, rotund gentleman with a great, hearty laugh and maintained a light, energetic touch to his directing. He also had a reputation for being a practical joker.

One day he shared the story of an open house he had on his horse ranch in Los Gatos. Plumbing had to be repaired, and, unfortunately had not been completed, so he had a fancy outhouse repaired and decorated.

Among his guests were two rather elderly neighbor ladies, who, of course, were directed to the outhouse when needed. What he did not tell them was that he had had a sound system installed in the depths, so that when anyone sat down, a loud voice would holler, "Can't you see we're paintin' down here?"

Dave Butler, obviously, loved practical jokes, but he had to admit, he felt a bit sad that he had forgotten two innocent ladies might have had a heart attack when confronted with this one.

When someone referred to a well known director, Dave Butler scoffed, "That man has the heart of a grapenut."

Dave Butler liked a comedy bit I did in the Kay Kaiser film, and when he learned that RKO had dropped my option, he said, "Ridiculous. But don't worry. I'm making a film with Bing Crosby at Universal Studios which will be a lot better studio for you than RKO. I'll find something for you to do in it. It's with Bing and Gloria Jean, a lovely little child actress and singer. I'll tell them to put you under contract and they will."

And they did. The movie was *If I Had My Way*.

There followed three or four years at Universal of bits and small parts in big films and starring parts in low budget films (B–pictures they were called). I played the lead in three or four Johnny Mack Brown westerns and enjoyed his warm and courteous manner, as well as learning to mount a horse, back away from the hitching post and gallop away. My co-actors had said, "Katie, when the horses hear the click of the take number and the director yelling, 'Action!' the horses know what to do. Just keep your hands on the reins and hang on!"

I enjoyed the Westerns with Johnny Mack Brown, a gracious gentleman; and especially felt rewarded playing the lead in the B–pictures I made with Donald Woods, who became a very good friend. But my spirit, my energy, was not in making films or persisting in moving from starlet to star. The sparkle in my personal firmament was getting ready to be married.

From my mother's perspective, I married much to soon. I wouldn't be free, after marriage, she would say, to pursue either my career in the movies, or go back to school and fulfill my other dream, closer to my father's heart — medicine, psychology — writing. It was assumed, in those days, that married life, for a woman, would close the doors to an independent life outside the walls of one's home. Deeper and never spoken, I realized later, my marriage would leave my mother without a life, without a reason for being, which, since my father's death, was caring for me.

In spite of the threat of abandonment, of misgivings about my chosen life partner, once my intentions were firmly announced, Mother dropped all arguments and criticisms, all pursed lips and doubt-filled silences, and set herself with her abundant energy to helping me get ready,

The only spoken disappointment she expressed was that I wouldn't have a Big Wedding!

"Katya, you didn't graduate from high school. You didn't graduate from college. And now you are not having a big wedding!"

This seemed inconsequential and impractical to me, monumentally disappointing to my mother. I was not pregnant. It was just that there was not that much money to invest in unnecessary showmanship. I had been helping my husband-to-be financially, a reality not uncommon among show business folk and wives of medical students; troubling to my mother. I had felt for Hugh and his long struggle to support his mother and young sister. How could I spend large sums of money on frivolities. The generosity of sharing what one had with deserving others, my father's attitude, no doubt, faded before custom, in my mother's mind. Never in her life did she get to put on a big production for me. And she would have done it so well — bells, blossoms, gloriously sweeping bridal gown, candles, towering cake and all.

She gave up this dream with gentle grace. She set to work finishing the handwork, the crocheted table cloth and bedspread, the embroidered dish towels, hurriedly trying to fill the "chest of hope" she had for her only daughter. Every now and then, she would look up from her needle work and say, "Oh, Katya, it is too bad you can't have a big wedding".

The powers-to-be at Universal were upset with me that I was marrying. Unwed starlets were much tastier fodder for publicity. And astonishing to them, I refused an offer that would have been a mint's worth of publicity.

Not many weeks before our simply planned ceremony, the publicity man, who had named Jean Harlow the Blond Bombshell, came to me with an astonishing offer. Gregory La Cava was making a film at Universal, *Unfinished Business* with Irene Dunne. He had cast me in a small role as Irene Dunne's sister. The script called for a wedding scene, in which Miss Dunne's sister was married. Why couldn't it be a real — not just a reel — wedding?

"Just think of the publicity for you — and for the film!"

I was shocked. Half-thoughts, objections, tumbled around in my brain.

"I — I couldn't possibly. We — Hugh and I, don't even have an apartment yet."

Answer, "We'll find you one and furnish it for you completely."

Objection, "I — I would like to have my brother Roland, who is a minister, perform the ceremony, and he is miles away in Willmar, Minnesota."

Solution. "We'll fly him in. No problem."

I said I'd think about it.

Hugh and I on the set of *Unfinished Business,* starring Irene Dunne.

It didn't take me long. To me a marriage ceremony was a sacred ritual, not a bit of entertainment for publicity purposes. Inside my mind and soul, there was no doubt. My mother supported me easily. Hugh knew it had to be my decision, and let the idea go.

La Cava let it go as well. The studio did not. It may have been that and my reluctance to do other things for publicity purposes that cooled them to me as a rising starlet. It is possible, of course, that I really wasn't star material!

It didn't occur to me to thank the studio and the publicity man, who was a red-headed, very gentle and unassuming human being, for wanting to support the film, my career, as well as his own.

The night before my very small wedding — to be attended by my mother, Uncle Jake and Aunt Emmeline, two cousins, my future mother-in-law and sister-in-law, the groom and me — after I had gone wearily and anxiously to bed, I heard the scuffle of slippered feet coming into the living room towards my pull-down bed. I sat up, turned on the light. There stood my mother, in a thin pink nighty, nervously finishing the braid of her long, beautiful hair.

"Katya. May I sit down?"

Great tenderness toward her filled my bring. She was doing so well with her disappointments, I knew, trying valiantly to fulfill my desires, dampening the fires of her own.

I patted the bed beside me. She sat down. She had drawn the braid around in front of her nighty. She looked like a vulnerable child.

"Katya, I want to tell you something tonight. Before your wedding. It's coming so soon. Much too soon. I was hoping you would wait until you were twenty-five or six before you married. So we'd have several more years together before I let you go."

"But", she said, genuine acceptance in her voice, "it isn't working out that way. So you know I wish you and Hugh the very best God can give you. You deserve it. I want to give you my blessing now, in our last night before you are a wife. I know Daddy Hohn would give his blessing, and so now, I too, my darling daughter."

She reached for me then, and hugged me tightly. Tears were on both our faces when we let each other go.

I thought she was finished with her simple words of blessing. But she wasn't. There was more. She fingered her braid as she stumbled on. I couldn't imagine what more there could be at this late hour.

"I want to say something else," she continued, "something only a mother can say. And it's hard. I don't know how to say it. I told you about my wedding night. How scared I was. How I didn't know anything, and your daddy had to tell me, and he was so thoughtful and kind."

I reached for her hand, to tell her with mine that she didn't really have to go on. But she needed to get it all out. She would go on, though it tore her in two.

"Well, my dear daughter, I don't have to tell you about life, intimate relations and such. You young people know so much more about these things than we did in those days. But I have to tell you — you see — I have to say before you marry that I hope you —. Well, you see, your father was so patient all the time and I believe Hugh will be, too — but . . ." The words were tumbling out now. "But you see, it was my fault, really, that we didn't — that I didn't — well, enjoy intimate relations as much as I could have — should have. I mean, if I weren't so tired all the time and didn't work so hard keeping house — cooking — cleaning, even though your father helped me a lot — still I worked all the time. Housework isn't that important, really, you see. So I hope you won't do as I did and get too tired to really be with Hugh. You see? You understand? My dear daughter?"

I thought I couldn't breathe, much less respond in any other way than to take her in my arms again in silent embrace. The gulf between our experiences was so great there was nothing I felt I could or wanted to say. But we were joined together in a way we had not been for a long time.

My mother, with the sure, maternal instinct so strongly within her, had made the effort to join with me, mother and daughter, in a holy ritual of preparation. It was the most honest and detailed she could give. In a way, it was even deeper than the initiation ceremony we shared for my first menstruation.

And so, Hugh Beaumont and I were wed the 13th of April, Easter Sunday, 1942. The simple ceremony was conducted (softly breathed would be a better description) by Allan Hunter, an amazing human being, who became a beloved friend and mentor for Hugh and for me, and for whom we named our eldest son, Hunter Beaumont.

Mother had prepared an elegant breakfast for us and our guests, and after that special meal, we retired to a small house we had rented. Publicity photographers met us at the door, took pictures and left.

Now, Hugh and I were together in a new way. Our wedding night was much like many I had read and heard about — mixed. Instead of rejoicing in each other in newly-wedded bliss, we each worried about our parents. Hugh worried about how he could continue to support his mother and sister now that he was a married man, with future children very likely. My career was not exactly on fire and his was lurching from one "short subject" to another, with long emptiness between. But, Hugh's mother went back to Long Beach with his young sister, Gloria, who would be with her at least until she finished high school. Emmeline and Jake and my cousins had each other. My mother was alone.

When June arrived with a burst of bloom in California, my mother closed the apartment we had shared and flew back, alone, to Minnesota, to Camp Laf-a-Lot. This was a place where she had neighbors; not next door, to be sure, but near enough to enjoy some things together. Most of the hours of the day and night, however, she would once again be alone.

Chapter Sixteen

Hugh's and my honeymoon didn't take place until late that summer, because my "lay off" period from Universal Studios was not available to me until that time. I was filming something, but can't remember just what it was. "Lay off" was an annual period from three to six weeks. I was given two weeks for this period.

The timing was perfect for our belated honeymoon, because my dream was for the two of us, and our dog, Rough, to travel by car to Minnesota. It would be Hugh's very first experience "north of the Mason-Dixon line" and my first since I left Minnesota, four and a half years ago. Hugh would meet my brothers, Roland and Win, and at last get to see and know Camp Laf–a–Lot, my childhood paradise.

I was sleepless with excitement for weeks before our trip. Hugh was curious, somewhat skeptical, but graciously accepting of my passionate desire to share my Northwoods with him. We traveled much too fast to get there, and drove too many hours without stopping. But arrive, we did, in the southwestern part of Minnesota.

As soon as we had crossed the border at Worthington, Hugh opened the car window, and shielding his eyes with his hand, peered at the surroundings.

"Where's the lake?" he asked, teasingly.

I'd never been to Worthington before and had no idea where the first lake in the state might be.

To my gratitude and amazement, there it was — a Minnesota blue lake right beside the highway, with a lovely white-sailed sailboat skimming gently through Sky Blue Water!

Triumph! My state had met the first test. Even Rough, our pit bull, stood up in the back seat and wagged his cropped tail.

Our first stop was Willmar, where my brother Roland was minister of the First Methodist Church. I don't think Hugh had ever been up close to a minister before, so meeting Rollie was a great, wonderful surprise. We visited, enjoyed Margy, Rollie's wife, and their three-year-old bright and charming daughter, Sally. I held the baby, Bonnie Marie, in my arms. We had dinner and gratefully accepted the invitation to go to bed and enjoy a good night's sleep before heading Up North.

Hugh and Rollie seemed to enjoy one another so much, Hugh asked if my brother would like to go with us up north to Lake Pokegama. He would, indeed. And so it was that I sat in the back seat with Rough, and Hugh and Rollie shared the front seat, totally engaged in bright conversation all the way to Grand Rapids. That was wonderful from my point of view, because it gave Hugh an opportunity to learn about the theology, philosophy, and values with which I had been brought up from someone other than me, and closer to Hugh's age. And Rollie was not only very bright and open-minded, but he had a wonderful, pixie-like sense of humor.

Mother had graciously gone to Crookston for a visit with old friends, so that Hugh and I could enjoy a time alone on our honeymoon at Camp Laf–a–Lot. My brother Win had paneled the cabin with pine paneling, covered the tar paper with log siding and Flo, his wife, had everything clean and neat and welcoming.

The very next day, Rollie and I took Hugh fishing. My brother and I took turns rowing the boat. I'll never forget the sight of Hugh, his feet braced against the transom, knees to chin, lifting his rod way up in the air, reeling and lifting, reeling and lifting, responding to his first hefty bite as though he were catching a marlin. It was so funny. I wish with all my heart I had film of Hugh Beaumont's first engagement with a fresh water, one-pound Northern Pike.

He, Hugh, was hooked! We decided that when the time was right, we would look for property in northern Minnesota, a place we could call our own and have the children we would plan for some day be able to spend their summers in this northern wonderland.

Our first child, Hunter, arrived, unplanned, April 23, 1943, slightly over a year after Hugh's and my marriage. I hadn't realized how easily I became pregnant; but when I discovered I was, awe and wonder filled my being. Hugh was less than enthusiastic, but accepted the reality with gentlemanly grace.

I have to admit now, in this my eighty-sixth year, that it was only in pulling back the camera of my mind, and really seeing myself in those young years, that I realized how naive and insensitive I was about Hugh's reluctance to be a parent. The responsibility for his young sister and his mother, whose health was not at all good, weighed heavily upon him. His motion picture career was staggering along, and after such a dramatic start, my own career was limping, certainly not leaping! Income to support three women, a mother, a sister, a wife, and then children, I understand now, must have been a heavy burden. Would he have to give up his acting aspirations to support us?

These thoughts did not occur to me then and once my first three months of nausea had passed, I enjoyed my pregnancy with feelings of deep satisfaction. Sitting in the bath tub and watching my tummy roll with new life, I was incredulous. How could all this be happening all on its own — new life, growing within me, without that little entity, the little "I" called the ego, doing anything at all about it, except watch my diet!

My mother had willingly agreed to come be with me during the last weeks of my pregnancy and help me after the baby had arrived and that knowledge was comforting.

She was there with me fully when my first child was born, from the last prenatal weeks to a few weeks after delivery. However, during the final, countdown days of my pregnancy, my mother had gently insisted that when the moment came for me to go to the hospital, Hugh only, should accompany me. Ahead of her time, she believed it was the husband's privilege and responsibility to share the birth experience.

"Christian was wonderful," my mother had told Hugh, "kept beside me every step of the way, and then was left alone when I went into the delivery room." That didn't seem quite right to either of us.

Mother waited at home for the call that our first-born, Hunter, had arrived, healthy and sound, as was I. She was grateful we had all come through without complications, but had known in her heart, she said, that everything would "come out" just fine.

(Hugh and I were fortunate to have had an unusually progressive obstetrician who allowed Hugh to be in the delivery room to experience what few expectant fathers at that time had been allowed to share. The small hospital was agreeable).

Mama was right about my Hohn hips, too. I was built to have children, so could remain conscious and cooperative all during labor when the doctor instructed me to "Push!"

Both my mother's story about my own birth as well as her command to have no medication, as well as stories of my paternal grandmother who was a midwife in Germany, came to me in those hours.

Grandmother Hohn, according to the story, got up out of bed after childbirth (how long after, I do not know) and traveled by sleigh in the snow to deliver another woman's baby. Her spirit and my mother's filled my being. I found myself actually praying. If God, the Creative Spirit, was anywhere, I instinctively felt he would be present at the birth of a child. When the time came for the episiotomy and the doctor used the word "cut", I willingly accepted the medication. The last thing I remember was the ring of laughter around me.

Later, cozied in my hospital room, with baby Hunter in my arms, Hugh told me what the laughter was all about. Apparently, as I was fading out from the medication, I managed to say, "I am now exploring the realms of the unknown!" I only wish I had been fully awake to hear my own lofty utterance!

My mother (and father, too) were instinctively right, and ahead of their time, to feel that fathers needed to be a more active and real part of the birth experience. As far as Hugh and I were concerned, this was clearly true. After Hunter's birth, Hugh felt drawn to him in a way he had not anticipated. He cradled him in his arms, kissed him on the cheek, before he gently and reluctantly placed him beside me in the hospital bed.

Once we were settled in at home, Hugh burped his son, changed his diapers, laughing at the productive, smelly mess, walked the floor with him when he fussed, and proudly laid him in his baby basket when he finally fell asleep.

When Hugh realized that the difference in ages between his much younger sister and himself was too great, he willingly agreed to have another child; and September 27, 1945, our daughter Kristan was born.

On May 9, 1949, Mark, our last child arrived, unplanned, but welcomed. Now, our family seemed to me to be complete — a boy — a girl — a boy. Little Kristy had wanted a sister, but when I called her on the phone and told her the new born was a brother, not a sister, she sweetly, softly said, "It's okay, Mama."

In the first few weeks after the birth of my first-born, my own Mama had challenged the way I handled my baby, but not at all fiercely. Inexperienced and Dr. Bundeson-bound young mother that I was, I forced myself into torturous schedules — six A.M. — (wake the baby at six!) ten A.M. — two P.M. and on, until the twenty-four hour cycle was complete.

No one in my world believed in motherly instinct in those days. My own mother gently encouraged me to breast feed as a healthy, wondrous experience for both infant and mother. But because of inner conflict about this fundamental right and privilege of infants and mothers, my breasts would not give down, and I gave up. All one needed to know about parenting could be found in books. Doctors knew best at that time. The wisdom of nature and of the ages bowed down to objective authority. Breast feeding was time consuming and unscientific. How could you know how many ounces of milk the baby was getting, if you couldn't see the ounce mark on the bottle?

Mama shook her head at these newfangled ideas and let it go. She let me find my own way. She helped me boil bottles and diapers, and sterilize every inch of equipment, let the baby cry when the inscribed feeding time had not yet arrived. She gave in without further protest of my furious ways, setting aside her own instinctive casualness.

I feel sure now that my first-born would have cried less and been more content had I trusted my mother's instinctive wisdom. I can't believe what I am remembering now, but one time when mother walked into the room, with the edge of the bottle nipple in her fingers, I sent her back into the kitchen to re-boil the rubber nipple and hold it out it to me with sterilized tongs! Of course, now it seems so ridiculous one has to laugh, but imagine my mother, and especially my first-born son, living within the aura of such anxiety.

We all survived those days, and as I relaxed my anxious behavior, I began to delight in my parenting. Each of the children were distinct personalities — grave, reflective Hunter, sparkling, dancing Kristy, and extroverted, love-everybody Mark. As the years flowed by we had our normal parent-child conflicts and concerns, but none of the three caused us major difficulty. My gratitude for my children and what they brought into my life, is deep and abiding.

◦—◦ Chapter Seventeen ◦—◦

DURING THOSE YEARS, I said goodbye to my film career. After Universal dropped my option, I did a few freelance things, one film with Hugh, *Blonde For A Day*. After that lusterless performance, I lost the interest and determination it takes to persist in pursuing a film career, and let it go.

I went back to school, instead, to "finish my education" at last. I had decided that going into the teaching profession was the fastest and best way to add to the family budget and still have time in the summer to go back to the Northwoods of Minnesota. Hugh had fallen in love with the North Country, and I longed for my children to experience what had meant so much to me most of my life before Hollywood.

During those years waiting to have the financial ability to purchase our own paradise in northern Minnesota, I graduated from Los Angeles State College, having traveled daily by street car to Vermont Avenue. I employed a baby sitter for Mark and arranged my student schedule so that I could be home before Hunter and Kristy arrived from their school. I don't remember how long this arrangement lasted, but I continued seeking my teaching credential and a Master of Arts Degree at the State College in Northridge.

Just before my last semester at Northridge State, I received a call from Jessica Ryan, wife of actor Robert Ryan. Robert and Jessica had been cofounders of the Oakwood School, on Moorpark in North Hollywood. That most unusual Elementary School had been founded on Quaker principles (Jessica had a Quaker background). The school had an exhausting and troubling beginning and was now looking for a teacher to replace one who had resigned.

I had not finished my practice teaching, but Jessica was in a glow about their new director, Miss Marie Spottswood, who had retired as the director of the Fieldstone Elementary School in Riverdale, a suburb of New York. Although this incredible woman had retired, she responded to Robert Ryan's plea to come to California and help the struggling school really get on its feet. After listening to Jessica's excitement about Miss Spottswood, I responded warmly, and agreed to make an appointment to meet the extraordinary Marie Spottswood. I'd worry about the practice teaching later.

Miss Spottswood was all, and more, than Jessica Ryan had described. She was a charming, grey-haired, warm, but dignified woman with the most beautiful diction I had ever heard. When she talked about her attitude toward children and her philosophy of education, I was enthralled. I was equally pleased with the kind of questions she asked me. I held my breath, hoping she would offer me the job, even though I did not as yet have a credential.

We seemed to have struck a chord with one another, because when she asked me if I had any more questions and I answered no, she held out her hand and said, "I'd be most pleased if you would work with me teaching the Fifth and Sixth grades. I don't know if that arrangement would qualify for practice teaching, but I would be more than willing to provide the powers that be with whatever information about you they need. Since we will be sharing the job, we could work it out so that you could attend school to finish your education."

"Finish your education." Those words were an echo of my father's words to me, so many years ago! How could that remarkable, gracious woman know what a powerful message they communicated to me. No need to go home and "think it over."

I was hired, and there followed a time of joy and fulfillment, as I learned from Miss Spottswood and took over the classroom by myself after the first year. My supervisor at Northridge saw to it that I was excused from my remaining practice teaching. With this flexible arrangement I went on to graduate from Northridge State with a major in education, and would be able to go back "Up North" to Minnesota during the summers, when the time came and we could find a place there.

The heart and soul of Oakwood was based on the social studies program, which could be described as a comparative cultures curriculum with artistic activity as the avenue of learning. The children spent an entire year immersed in a culture, starting with the Native Americans, and moving on to Ancient Greece, the Vikings, the Middle Ages, the Chinese, the Egyptians. They sang, and danced, made pottery, paper, learned a to use the ink stick and brush to paint and do calligraphy, learned to put together an octavo-sewn book — all manner of activities that grew out of these differing cultures, which had contributed to our own. Miss Spottswood would often repeat a phrase of a well-known educator, Lucy Sprague Mitchell, "The work of the hand illumines the mind." Another saying of Miss Spottswood's I remember so well when the children had to wait for something, "I don't want the children to miss the delights of longing." Do children today known anything of these delights?

One of the bits of genius of the Oakwood approach was that this hands-on activity was called "Work Period," giving the word "work" a value the children cherished. Mornings were spent learning the "three R's," reading, writing,

All three of the "me" that I hardly knew! "What would my father think?"

Left: A publicity shot for *Love, Honor, and O Baby!*

Below: Kathryn starred with Edward Everett Horton and Donald Woods in the comedy, *Sandy Steps Out*

Left: A publicity shot for *Pic! Magazine,* 1941.

arithmetic; and these were conducted in very small groups of no more then eight children.

My delight in this educational approach was boundless. I loved the research I needed to do to enrich the cultural studies. My love and respect for, as well as enjoyment of the children deepened, and influenced the way I related to my own children. I learned from my teaching experience at Oakwood that in working with, living with, the young, it is far better to encourage them to "unfold rather than force them into a mold." (Frances Wickes, *The Inner World of Childhood*)

Remembering my father's love of poetry, and memorizing reams of it from my earliest years, I wanted my own children, and the children I taught, to experience the poetic world. And so, one piece of their "homework" was to find a poem, memorize it, and bring it to class in the morning, when we would begin the day sharing their bit of memorization.

The experience was unforgettable — and astonishing. At first, they teased me by memorizing the most mundane of rhymes, silly limericks, jokes in rhyme. I accepted it all without comment, and laughed with them.

The astonishment came, when their morning offerings gradually changed, grew deeper, more truly poetic. The boys discovered Lew Sarret, some of Tennyson; the girls, Emily Dickinson, Edna St. Vincent Millay. Poetry, the music of words, seemed to open a part of their being, the feeling and intuitive aspects of their natures. And they soon wanted to write poetry of their own. When John F. Kennedy was assassinated, many of the children wanted to write poems about death, and their pain and puzzlement seemed to be eased.

I will never forget my experience of teaching at the Oakwood School. It changed and deepened my awareness of many, many things and released my own creativity. With a generous grant from Elizabeth Harmon Schappert, one of the founding parents of Oakwood, I was able to take the time to write the curriculum of the school, and I completed six cultural studies before I left California and moved back to my home state, Minnesota.

I believe it was the depth of the social studies, the reading of myths and legends, that opened the children to their own depth, and opened me to the potential depths of the children.

They began to come to me during recess and after school, wanting to share their night time dreams and the day time experiences that troubled them. I decided, then, I needed to go back to school to prepare myself to become a licensed psychologist.

And I did. Miss Spottswood arranged my time at the school, so that I could attend classes, many of them at night.

I cannot say I learned a great deal from my academic studies of educational psychology — not as much as I learned from observing and working with Marie Spottswood; and certainly not as much as I learned during my supervised work at Footlighters Child Guidance Clinic, associated with the Hollywood Presbyterian Hospital. This experience was the culmination of my work seeking my Master's Degree in Educational Psychology and then becoming licensed as a psychologist.

After a time of observing, I was allowed to conduct therapy with the children, and during that time, the value of their doing art work as a revelation of their inner life, as well as therapy for them, became abundantly clear.

During the months of my supervision, we had the privilege of working directly with Dora Kalff, a Jungian analyst who was in the United States from Switzerland and offered the clinic a generous amount of her time. She had just finished her book *Sand Play* and gave each of the therapists individual time observing our work and sharing the insights she had gained through her years of working with children.

As I silently watched the child search our shelves filled with hundreds of items from witches to spiders to heroes, fairies, monsters, put them in the trays filled with sand, studiously arrange and rearrange them, I was astonished. Their conflicts, fears and desires were revealed in an amazing way. I wanted to paraphrase what I had learned at Oakwood from "the work of the hand illumines the mind" to "work in the sand reveals the soul".

After I finished my required time of supervision, and received my Masters Degree, I was offered a part time position at the clinic. This was a continuing educational opportunity for me, offering friendships and professional exchanges on a daily basis. I fulfilled the required time for supervision, took the state exam, and was licensed as a psycho-therapist.

I was delighted, fulfilled, and soon gained enough confidence as a therapist to begin seeing children, and adults as well, in my home. I never once looked back with regret for having abandoned my film career.

Chapter Eighteen

DURING THOSE YEARS working as a teacher, psychotherapist, and homemaker, Hugh's career picked up enough that we could afford to look for and buy some property and build a simple cabin in the Northwoods. He had been doing some short subjects, commercials and military training films in Detroit, Michigan, and was offered a few minor parts in major films in a variety of studios in Hollywood.

Now we developed a pattern, a lifestyle, that allowed us to fulfill my desire, not only for me, but for my children. During the summer months, when Hugh would get a call for something to be filmed in Detroit, he would immediately cash in the airplane ticket the Detroit studio wired him. Then, we would quickly pack some bedding and clothes, empty the refrigerator, close the windows, pack the car, lock the doors and take off, speeding across the country, stopping over night only one time until we reached Grand Rapids, Minnesota, Hugh would drop me and the children off at Camp Laf–a–Lot on Lake Pokegama, where my mother received us with warm food and soft beds. He would then fly from Grand Rapids to Detroit in time for him to start filming.

After his return, the very next day, Hugh and I would head north, looking for property, remote, beautiful and affordable. During these searching days, I would leave the children with my mother, taking it for granted she would delight in having them to herself! Isn't that what grandmothers were for?

I don't remember how many years we followed this pattern, learning to travel light, with only Hugh and myself, our first two children, and two Golden Retrievers. Later, after Mark arrived and was old enough to become a dedicated hamster breeder, we brought the first cage of hamsters with us. That was when we realized hamsters were nocturnal animals and their squeaky exercising in their cage in the motel bathroom kept us awake most of the night!

The summer before Mark's birth in 1949, we finally found the special place, forty miles north of Grand Rapids, nine miles through the woods from Marcell, population ninety. We purchased the property from Old Mike, a hermit junk dealer who had moved into the swamp several miles from his tumbling down shack on the hill were we had hoped to build. He had already taken his forty (or more?) dogs into the swamp where he bragged about feeding them mostly flies and dead fish. Old Mike had been glad to sell because, in his own words, "There's gitten to be too many folks around, an' I's got me 'popity' a ways off, whar nobody kin bother me."

We called our place Lonesome Water after a poem Hugh especially loved, and the name seemed to fit our place. Clubhouse Lake lay to the south of the hill on which we planned to build our cabin. On the north a small lake named Little Lake, and a wandering stream connected the two lakes. To reach Lonesome Water, we drove through a large, beautiful stand of full-grown, lofty, majestic Norway pine.

One of the first things we had to do before we could start to build was to construct a rough plank bridge across the stream strong enough to carry construction material for our log-siding cabin. Before we built the bridge we had to drive through the shallow shore of Clubhouse Lake to reach our chosen cabin sight. We had a well dug, with a hand pump, and before too many weeks, we were able to move Up North and said a good-bye to my mother, leaving her alone once more.

During those years, there was never one complaint or word of protest from the children about the long trip from California, leaving friends there, or our "roughing it" lifestyle, once we moved into our first wilderness home. They delighted in the experience of running barefoot through the woods, picking blueberries, and wild raspberries, splashing in the stream, swimming in the lake.

The great variety of people we became close to in our Lonesome Water days added much to our lives there, and gave our children an opportunity to know and appreciate wonderful individuals very different from those we knew in Southern California.

A deep and abiding friendship developed with Joe and Irene Ruploski who had a mink farm beyond Lonesome Water on East Lake. They were a very dear and remarkable couple, who were available whenever I needed them when Hugh was gone and I was at Lonesome Water alone with the children. I only had to ring on the brake drum with a stove lid poker we had hung outside our cabin, and one or both of them would be there in moments. They were incredibly good with the children, letting Hunter help them feed the mink and the goats they kept for the healthy milk they provided. Hunter was diligent about helping me as well, pumping water, carrying it into the house, and helping me start the gasoline washing machine we had purchased and placed outside our cabin door next to the pump.

Irene and I, with little Kristy following us would creep through the woods, bent over, blueberry pail in one hand while the other parted the undergrowth to reach the abundant, luscious fruit and pop them by the handful into the pail, all the time discussing Plato and Aristotle and philosophical issues. Irene was an intelligent, self educated soul whose spirit gently influenced our days at Lonesome Water.

All the while, Kristy was busy picking, too. Now and then, she would join the conversation and say, "I'th pickin' blueberryth!" as she popped them in her mouth. Her lisp was a part of her charm at that age, and I had decided not to try and correct her and certainly not laugh when she spoke, but wait to see if she wouldn't outgrow the lisp naturally. And she did. (That approach does not fit every situation, I know).

Hunter and Mark kept busy building model boats and trying out their little motors in the lake. Or Mark would follow his big brother through the woods to help Joe with one of his forever present tasks.

Then, there was the Finlander who came to help us put up the cabin. Hugh had gone in to Marcell, the nearest town to our property, and located a Finlander named Oscar Karjala to help make the rough frame livable. Oscar would pull into the yard, park near the pump, get out of the car, pick up his lunch pail and knock on our door at precisely eight o'clock every morning!

Oscar was efficient and skilled, as well as scrupulously honest, which we learned was characteristic of the Finlanders who had settled the area. His language was well-spiced with epitaphs that slipped into his pronouncements as though they were a natural part of the English language, likely learned from sailors. "Goddam ting is rooked," he would say of the ridge pole old Mike had cut for us. But he put his frustration aside and struggled to raise the crooked pole into place. Its crookedness became a natural part of our Northwoods decor.

When we had settled in to our cabin, which we never got to finish on the inside, we learned about Rose and Ray Gravelle, who had a home on a nearby lake. Ray had been a taxi driver in the Twin Cities and wrote poetry. Rose had been a rodeo star in South Dakota. They moved to the Northwoods to get away from the noise and too-busy-ness of city life. Ray became a fishing guide and Rose kept her beautiful rodeo regalia and her handsome horse well groomed. They had a few cows, and it was from them we bought milk and cream.

They had a telephone, and because Hugh had to have some way to keep contact with his agent in California, since there were no telephone lines anywhere near our property, the Gravelles graciously offered to take and deliver long distance messages for us.

One warm summer day when Hugh was with us at Lonesome Water, we looked out across the stream to see a vision slowly, carefully crossing the rough plank bridge. Astride a magnificent horse in full leather and silver regalia, was Rose, also garmented in the splendor of her rodeo costume, complete with silver spurs and a broad brimmed hat whose silver bells tinkled and sparkled in the sun. It was Rose Gravelle, who had dressed especially for the occasion of delivering a telephone message to Hugh Beaumont from Hollywood!

We have never forgotten that vision.

There are many other visions that we Californians have never forgotten. They were an integral part of our shared desire to return to the northwoods, across the two thousand plus miles of the USA, every summer.

Our cabin had been built on the gentle hill overlooking the stream and the lake beyond, making it possible for the open sky, unobstructed by trees, to arch above us day and night. During the day, there always seemed to be a breeze that came off Clubhouse Lake before us, or Little Lake behind us.

We had spectacular views of storms rising, and then fading away. One time, after a downpour and the sun had come out again, the children and I went outside to see if there was a rainbow. We looked up — and there was not only one rainbow, but three! We clapped our hands in appreciation and jumped with joy!

Another time there were blue-black storm clouds in the east, and a golden globe of the setting sun in the west. These moments, insignificant as they may be, have stayed with my children all through the years. Again, my gratitude is boundless..

The time came, however, when we felt we had to leave Lonesome Water and find another place to be during the summer. At the persistence of lakeshore owners beyond us through the woods, the county pushed a road right through our property, only a few yards from the picture window that gave us such a stunning view of Clubhouse Lake. That, and thinking it would be good to be a bit closer to my mother, whose visits with us she looked forward to so much, gave us the incentive to put the property up for sale, and again, start our search for another summer home.

Chapter Nineteen

CLOSER TO MY MOTHER — YES. That was important to her, and to me, in a different way. Those earliest days, before the cabin was ready for the children and me to move in, Hugh would go on up to the cabin to help, and the children and I would stay with my mother, easing guilty feelings that plagued me for leaving my mother alone so much.

After my marriage, as soon as the weather settled into summer in Minnesota, Mother flew back to Camp Laf–a–Lot, and she had continued that yearly journey. That first year back in Minnesota, Hugh wrote a beautiful letter to her. This is her reply:

July 24, 1942
Dear Hugh,

Thank you so much for your very kind words in your letter. I did appreciate it so much. I think we both have reasons to be thankful for Kathy's life. Now you can see why I was so very selfish by not wanting to give her up. But such is life, what is one person's gain seems to be another's loss. I shouldn't really take it as a loss, but more of a gain in adding another member to the family. You no doubt can see though that it meant a great change in my life. It hurt so much to break up my home. I feel sometimes that wherever I hang my hat I must call home. Of course this isn't because of you taking Kathy, but ever since Daddy Hohn left, it isn't the same. Even here at camp it seems different.

Maybe I shouldn't write today. The weather is sort of gloomy and I don't feel so well. No time for writing letters!

With love, Mama Hohn

In all of the fifty-four letters I received from my mother in the first two years of my marriage, the child is clearly in conflict with the adult, the mature woman with the dependent, lonely, frightened child. I see her there in the lines, in between the lines.

I have saved most of my mother's letters. Why did I save them, arriving as they did with guilt producing regularity? They are, in may ways, the same letter, a quite detailed account of her daily life, what she did in and around her home, which was now centered, in the spring, summer and fall, in our old Camp Laf–a–Lot.

Activities there filled the empty hours for her, refinishing furniture, supervising well diggers, baking, sewing, doing all kinds of other handwork, coming and going across the country seeking a winter's nesting place. She stayed with her children, her sisters, friends, seeking a new place every fall, going where she was needed, if not always wanted.

Now, it meant a great deal to me to be able to exchange visits with my mother, not just to relieve my guilt, but to enjoy her food, to appreciate the special attention she gave to my daughter, Kristy.

One of our first summers at Lonesome Water, I was alone with the children. Hugh was either back in California, or in Detroit, working. We happened to be having the very worst wood-tick epidemic I had ever experienced. Every night, every inch of the children would have to be explored from head to toe, to find and remove those tiny, blood-thirsty insects they had collected. Our dog, Misky, a Black Labrador we had acquired from Joe and Irene and dearly loved, had so many wood-ticks, I couldn't possibly find and remove them all. He grew blue bubble gum enlargements on his ears and neck, filled with tick-blood, and I spent hours removing them with cotton dipped in kerosene.

One evening, for the first time in my life, I believe, I cursed the northwoods, and burst into tears.

My children, reversing roles, comforted me. That's when I knew it was I, not they, that needed a mother! We quickly stuffed our pajamas and toothbrushes into a bag, climbed into the car, and speedily drove the forty miles down to Grand Rapids, to Camp Laf–a–Lot. *And Mother!*

When we arrived, we climbed out of the car and hurried to the cabin. The door was locked! Mama was gone. Where, I had no idea. The grown-up me put on my thinking cap, as my parents used to say, and figured she was visiting a neighbor, or more likely, gone to town with one of them. Locked doors were not a usual thing for her. Unlocked doors were.

Unlocked doors. There was the answer. She had a small cabin built on the property, furnished with a bed, a small table, a ceramic potty, all ready for overflow company.

Exhausted and hungry, we found the door to the little cabin open, went in and flopped down on the bed, all four of us. Misky, our dog, smelled something and put his teeth into an unopened roll of salami, which he gave up reluctantly. Without a knife, without a prayer, we took turns biting hunks of salami and saved a bit for Misky. Our hunger was assuaged until my mother returned, overjoyed to see us, transferred us to the comfortable rooms in the larger cabin, kissed each of us, and left us to fall asleep.

Her just being there for me and my children quickened my realization, that at times in all our lives, everyone needs a *mother*. If she is there for us when we need her, we are blessed indeed.

None of our other visits to see my mother were as dramatic, and I unfortunately let my own need for her fall into unconsciousness; and instead, thought of our visits to my mother as being of most importance to her, and to my daughter, Kristan.

Kristan's father was probably more dedicated to being a good father to his sons than to his daughter, compensating, perhaps, for the wound of his own father's abandonment of him when he was a very young man.

One time, at Lonesome Water, Hugh planned to take Hunter and Mark, still a little boy, on a special fishing trip on Clubhouse Lake. Kristan wanted very much to go along. But no. There wasn't enough room in the boat, no, no, they would get their lines tangled. And they shoved off without her. I watched the failed transaction from the window of the cabin, my heart as broken as Kristy's. I watched her, standing there on the rough plank bridge that spanned the stream, enduring her grief alone. I was about to run down to her, to comfort her, and carry her in my arms up to the cabin to feed her something special, or read to her — anything to ease her pain. But just as I was about to turn around and run to the door, I saw her straighten her shoulders, rub her tears away with her small fists, and march with elegant, child-like determination up to the cabin. She grabbed a bamboo fishing pole propped against the cabin, marched back down to the bridge, plopped herself down on the plank, and stuck the fishing pole in the stream below!

My mother! Yes! I saw her in my very young daughter. This was my mother's spunk and determination. I said a swift thank you to both in my heart. So, the visits to my mother at Camp Laf–a–Lot were an occasion for mutual love and appreciation.

So it was that after putting our property northeast of Marcell up for sale we began our search for a place closer to Grand Rapids and Lake Pokegama. We wanted to be closer to my mother, but also wanted a secluded place that was protected from the invasion of unwanted roads and too close neighbors.

One unforgettable day in the summer of 1957, when I was in Minnesota with the children alone, the real estate agent with whom we had listed our property paid me a visit at Lonesome Water. He brought with him photographs and descriptions of a place only fourteen, not forty, miles from Grand Rapids that would surely fulfill our dream and our need for privacy.

"I've got it!" he declared, before he had even gotten out of his car. "This is it. An island! It just came on the market and is the perfect place for you. A thirty acre Island with only two dwellings and its gorgeous! Talk about privacy! You've just got to see it — today. It's called Balgillow, that means home of boys, I think, because the original owners were Scots and had a bunch of sons.

An island! That's got to be it, I thought, and hustled the children to get ready for the trip with the agent to go and see it, right away!

Our enthusiastic real estate agent, Steve, drove us all the way from Lonesome Water to lovely Lake Wabana, put a motor boat in the water, and slowly motored us around the most beautiful piece of property we had ever seen in our lives. The West End, high and mighty, was wooded with tall virgin Norway, white pine and cedar; the East End, with spruce, balsam, and birch; and there was a lovely bay with cattails and wild irises, water lilies and red-winged blackbirds chortling from reed to reed.

Tucked away on the East End, almost entirely hidden beneath damp undergrowth, were six or seven Showy Lady's Slippers, *Cypripedium Reginae*, shyly opening their beautiful pink and white moccasin-like blossoms to the June air. These lovely flowers were, and are, protected by the State of Minnesota from picking, touching, transplanting. On seeing them, I felt like kneeling down in the wet moss and saying "Thank You" to the Creator.

Miss Sebo, from whom we purchased the island, called the inhabitants of Balgillow Island, Keepers, because, in tune with Native American beliefs, two-legged humans could not be owners of land. So it was that during the years the Beaumont family were Keepers, we sheltered these precious flowers, and the small group grew, year by year, to a company of sixty or more.

Besides Lady's Slippers, there were many other lovely wild flowers, ferns, mosses, flowering shrubs, wild berries — and two buildings, erect and quite spacious, though badly in need of repair. Bats abounded. So did squirrel-chewed furniture and mattresses.

The Keeper before us was a former college professor, Miss Mildred Sebo, who had developed an unusual American Girl's Camp, with high ideals and lots of creative activity. She was deeply dedicated "to making the world a better place by making better women."

All three of the children wrote heartfelt "Dear John" letters to their father,

Left: Home in Van Noord Avenue, North Hollywood. Brother Win remodeled it for us. The photograph was taken for a feature article in *Ladies' Home Journal.*

Right: Lower Lodge — the tree covering the building blew down one stormy night.

Left: Mrs. Beaumont (Hugh's mother), Hunter, Kristan, Kathryn, and Mark.

Hugh's mother was 'Gammy' to the children and she loved our Northwoods.

expressing their enchantment with the Island "they had fallen in love with". They were insistent that we own it!

Did Hugh really have a choice? After one swift visit, he started exploring the possibility of purchasing the island. It was an amazing coincidence that Hugh had just been cast as Ward Cleaver, the father in the television series *Leave It To Beaver* that became such a popular and well-loved show. It would be the first time in our fifteen years of marriage that Hugh had a steady income, so he felt comfortable presenting the most fair asking price. Miss Sebo took a year to explore our suitability to be the next Keepers of Balgillow. She watched each episode of *Leave It To Beaver* and decided we were worthy of the honor.

And so, in the spring of 1958, the Beaumont family became the new Keepers of this magnificent piece of Mother Earth.

Our reception around the lake was amazingly warm and welcoming, and changed the tenor of our stay in the Northwoods. At first, the residents around the lake were dismayed that the new Keepers were from Hollywood, envisioning helicopters and speed boats roaring across the lake and swarming through the air, bringing guests for drunken parties to the Island.

One family ventured to visit us — tentatively, and became abiding friends. Another had a tea party to welcome us. Children and teenagers from around the lake soon invited our children to campfires, cookouts, treasure hunts. But not one neighbor was intrusive.

We quickly reciprocated. With the Island, we inherited a three-gallon, hand-cranked ice cream freezer, that took seventy-five pounds of ice and over two thousand cranks to freeze the incomparable homemade ice cream we made. Hunter and his Dad put up a volleyball net, and all the kids took turns playing volleyball and cranking the freezer.

In the Lower Lodge, the building close to the water, there was an old player piano, that no longer played electronically, but the kids had a lot of fun, plunking the broken keys and making up music so they could dance. Their parties sometimes lasted until the stars came out. Even when it got quiet in the Lower Lodge, we didn't feel we needed to check on them. Maybe our confidence was misplaced, but I guess we thought there was safety in numbers. Mark may have served, unknowingly, as chaperone. It was very different from Lonesome Water, indeed, but it came at the right time, because Hunter and Kristy were teenagers, and needed the companionship of others their own age. And because Mark was always included, he basked in the glow of dancing with the most beautiful girl on the lake!

Hugh was gone a great deal of the time, filming for the *Beaver* show, and it was during those days and weeks, I began to wonder what was happening — or not happening — to our relationship. I began to wonder if our separate careers, the different sets of friends we made, different interests, was causing the drifting apart, in spite of our mutual love of the Island, and our children. But these thoughts did not stay with me long, and it was many more years before I began to understand the depth of father-daughter projections on both our parts, a way of relating that began when we met, and made growing out of them difficult.

During Hugh's absence, I trusted and depended on my children. Their father and I had made an agreement with our three offspring that their "Work Period" would be in the morning hours, and the afternoon and evenings would be theirs to enjoy as they chose. This seemed to cause little resistance from Hunter and Kristy. Mark, the outgoing extrovert, was much more interested in deepening friendships around the lake thank in time consumed by leaf-raking, painting, and hauling water from the pump outside of the Lower Lodge, up the hill to our kitchen in the Upper Lodge. But he stuck to his promise with slow steps and deep sighs.

And so those island years rolled by with yearly summer trips to the place that enraptured us with its incredible beauty and deepened our bonding with our Earth Mother.

Chapter Twenty

AS FAR AS MY OWN EARTHLY MOTHER WAS CONCERNED, although our original idea was to find something closer to her, when we finally found and purchased the Island, she was no longer living on Lake Pokegama.

Before our move to Balgillow Island, Mama had been floating around here and there during the winter; Camp Laf-a-Lot during the brief summers. She was essentially unmoored, uncertain, but carrying on as best she could. In relationship to her, I am not proud of those years. They were not the same as the irritation of my adolescent years, but the relationship was taken for granted, and not truly appreciated. When I spoke to people about my early years, it was always my father I spoke about in worshipful tones.

It must have been fifteen or more years of the life Mama spoke of as vagabonding, before she began to express greater and firmer discontent with her winter wanderings and more burdened with caring for Camp Laf-a-Lot. It was time for a change.

My brother Win, the wanderer, had settled into a comfortable marriage and lifestyle. He became a skilled and artistic carpenter, and his remodeling of the cabin made old Camp Laf-a-Lot into the beautiful and highly saleable lake's edge home it had become. It seemed wise for mother to sell our childhood paradise so that she could build a place of her own in southern California where Win's and my families were both living and where Win could build a smart, modern duplex for her.

I assumed, wrongly, that the pain of this separation would be very great. Not so. The time had come. My mother sold the property, which it had now become, no longer a home. She packed her things and moved with hardly a tear.

Now, at long last, she had a place she could call her own and near to at least two of her children and their families. Now she could relax, settle in, join a church and love and care for her neighbors. The only thing she complained about was the eucalyptus trees in her yard. They were incredibly dirty from her point of view.

"Katya," she would say, almost every time I saw her, "you know those dirty trees are good for nothing but making a mess! Do you know they do five messy things? They lose their leaves, dirty the sidewalk, drop those little buttons, their bark and — they spit! Some kind of sticky oil. And they rattle in the wind."

The hostile trees and increasingly noisy traffic past her duplex finally neces-
sitated another move which was accomplished with relative ease. She made
friends easily with her new neighbors, joined another church and adjusted
quickly to her fresh, convenient single dwelling, which my brother Win had
also built. I was grateful and relieved that my mother seemed to make the adjustment so easily.

"What shall we do about Mother?" That question had plagued my brothers
and me for years. We assumed, then, that we were the ones that had to make
the decision, because our mother was not capable of making it on her own.
But we never once sat down together with her to talk about it.

Before the Women's Movement, many others, women in general, were
thought of and treated in the same way. They were patronized in sentimental
Mother's Day acknowledgements, then railed against in mother-hover-smoth-
er diatribes, mourned for, longed for in clamorings for stay-a-home mothers
and family values. Women who dared venture into the masculine world, endured the begrudging, often hostile remarks of the men who felt forced to
make space beside them, calling them, behind their backs, such epitaphs as
"hen doctors".

It must be difficult for young women of today to really believe that such attitudes were prevailing, and to appreciate the valiant struggle that many women
had to make to achieve their honored and needed place in the world outside
the home. And church.

Back then, I was unconsciously caught in the same stifling net, my father the
King; my mother, not the Queen, but the faithful servant.

Anger at myself is rising as I remember my attitude in those days when I
thought I understood it all and had no wisdom. Is this Woman-Spirit rising?
Inwardly, I now protest the way I thought of my mother back then, the way
society thought of women, my self included — needed and competent in the
home, the church, the farm — inferior and helpless in the world outside.

Flashbacks of the days of my father's illness burst into my brain. Where was
my mother in all this?

She was climbing the stairs with nourishment, changing the sheets, caring
for the two she loved deeply in the only way she believed she knew.

Did the community worry about my mother in those days? Come to the house
just to see her, to comfort, praise or relieve her? Was all of her steadfast care
completely taken for granted — that's what a woman, a wife, a minister's wife
was for?

It was as though all of the loving light of concern and admiration was focused on my father, and my mother carried on in the wings, while my father was on the stage. Does my memory fail me? Did anyone ever say to me, "Your mother is a woman of remarkable courage — the way she carries on — her indomitable spirit?" When she did the human thing and cried, she was "feeling sorry for herself." When she was cross and irritable, "just see how Christian suffers and never complains."

Did she ever seethe at the injustice of it all? I never heard her complain during that time, ever. Oh, before he became so ill, she complained that my father criticized her for spending so much on butter at Christmas, "but then, he eats the cookies!" she would say. And I remember her complaining about me, that I didn't help her enough in the kitchen, which was true, didn't wash my stockings every night, sassed her back when she fussed at me.

In those adolescent days of my life, we seemed to be always in conflict, alienated from one another. Gone were the memories of her being there for me in so many sensitive ways in the earthy round of my daily life. Instead, it seemed as though we were in a strange kind of competition. Which one of us would capture and hold the adoration of my father, the seat of honor beside him, up there in the realm of the spirit?

Was Freud right that competition for the father's love was part of the mother-daughter rivalry? Or had Carl Jung seen more deeply into the realm of the human psyche and realized parent-child relationships had deeper, universal roots.

Because of unease about my marriage, I had recently begun work with a Jungian analyst and was just beginning to be aware that something more powerful than mother-daughter rivalry was stirring within me. Realizations about my mother were coming alive. I began to see her in a new light. I began to listen to her story, and it became a more vital part of my own.

After the last of her children had married and left home, and the core of her mothering was gone, Mama felt expendable, a burden. She often said, and meant it, "I do not want to be a burden."

What if the feistiness in her nature, expressed in her fierce defense of the children at the Orphan's Home, had had a wider arena, the problem of child abuse and neglect, for example. What if the courage she showed in living alone at the lake, without close neighbors, fighting bats and cold, putting up with the outdoor "biffy"; as well as her efficiency in managing continuous entertaining, cooking and baking for twelve to fourteen people on the tiny cook stove at the lake, to say nothing of all that she did for the churches my father served — what if these skills had been applied some place in the outer world. The world needs mothering, domesticity, and my mother's abundant good humor could have brought lightness and joy to dark situations in many places.

She took care of a nephew during his illness until his death and stayed with her niece through the days of grieving. She went as caregiver for needy relatives, whenever and wherever she was called. But for these expressions of love, she was paid only with room and board and gratitude.

I realize with shock that my mother was only fifty-eight years old when I married. Today, in these late to come about Women's Movement years, she would undoubtedly, I believe, have felt young enough to pursue a new career, or develop an undeveloped talent, and been encouraged to do so. I smile when I think of the possibility of Mother getting involved in some Little Theater, mothering the troupe, mending costumes, bringing them coffee, something to eat.

With this idea popping into my head, I faintly remember my mother's saying to me in her first days in Hollywood, "An actress, my very own daughter. I myself, Anna Marie Rockel Hohn, wanted to run away from home and join Chautauqua when I was younger than you are now. I loved being Simon Peter's mother-in-law in the Methodist Conference play and coming out on the stage, raised from the dead, with my hair flowing down my back and hearing the audience gasp with wonder and surprise. And I loved being Martha Custis Washington for the church supper during the Washington Centennial, and singing 'Charlie is me darlin'' for the church bazaar. And curling my hair in ringlets for the Spring Festival.

"Maybe this love of performing is in you as it was in me. I'd never tell it to anyone, but maybe you got your talent from me, after all. You got your brains from your father, his kind of mind. But it was me who got you performing, not your father. I taught you to speak pieces when you were only four for Sunday School and church and taught you the pantomime for 'I think when I read that sweet story of old — ' You are my daughter, after all. You always loved speaking pieces and declaiming. And maybe you'll make some real money as an actress, and we won't have to think about it all the time."

How could I possibly have forgotten this stunning declaration of my mother? Suddenly, laughter bubbled up inside of me and I laughed out loud all by myself. In that instantaneous moment I realized that I, myself, had fallen into the trap! It was I who had cast my own mother in the inflexible role of the domestic, nurturing provider. Typecasting, indeed! Was this all my projections onto my mother could imagine? I was stunned at my own unconscious inflexibility.

My all-by-myself laughter fades, and turns into numbing sadness as this realization comes to me. When I try to imagine what would have happened to my mother — to me, if I'd had the awareness and appreciation of my mother's latent talent to urge her to give it a try in the movies in Hollywood. She might have joined a little theater, stepped out onto the stage, find an agent? If she could hold the attention of Mr. W. C. Fields for an entire afternoon, she certainly might have captured film audiences. She, not I, was the natural!

Would my mother have been too frightened to venture forth, she who had no fear of bats or storms or beggars off the streets? Or, at root, did she really not want to do more than to continue with the known, making a home for her children; now, especially me, her only daughter, warm, secure, nourishing. Did she just want to be genuinely honored for that task as she basked in reflected glory, as she had always done with her husband, my cherished father.

As it was, the pain of loss and letting go was something she endured in solitude. Her soul's maturing went unrecognized by me, or my brothers, until very close to the end. And I am deeply sorry that this is so.

Now, in the next few years when my mother had settled in a home of her own — not a parsonage, not a summer home — a profound shift in our relationship took place. There seemed to be a letting go on both our parts. Tense, mutual expectations of each other gave way to genuine acceptance, and this is still a wonder to me, pure delight.

Busy as I was with family, teaching, working as a therapist, I did not see my mother as often as she would have liked. But when we were together, it was gentle and good. We ran errands, shopped, which she loved, got ready for holidays, did some reminiscing. There were few confidences exchanged, but an easy, quiet companionship developed between us. Now we were like the dearest of friends, very different in temperament, but bound by a long, shared history and mutual love and respect.

Mother kept her small house immaculately clean, gardened, went to church, enjoyed her neighbors and tried to control her high blood pressure with diet and vigorous lawn mowing.

Once in a while she would call me on the telephone, not quite able to wait for my weekly visit.

"Katya?"

"Yes, mother. I'm here."

Then would come a recital of all she had accomplished that day, and we would chat comfortably about this and that, until, "My Katya. I'm lonely."

A wave of compassion washed over me. "Yes, Mother, I can well imagine that you are."

There had been no demand in her voice. I felt no adrenaline rush of guilt, no need to reassure her, make suggestions, or scold. The statement of what she was feeling at the moment was a simple statement of fact. No need on her part to explain it all, no need for me to rescue her just then. She knew how busy my life was and that I genuinely looked forward to sharing lunch with her on our appointed day.

"I love you, Mother."

"I know you do. I love you, too. Just wanted to hear your voice. Say hello to Hugh and the children. See you Thursday."

Coming as I did from a deep, but never pious, religious tradition, I am wary of such words as Grace. I had never used it before. But when it comes to my relationship with my mother, after the deep identification with my father, of trying to be perfect and knowing it all, there is no other word to describe it. This newness of being for both of us, seemed to come from a source outside myself and had little to do with will. It is simply that my mother and I were bonded in a new way. I do not need or want to analyze, or try intellectually to understand it. I simply want to remember its mystery with wonder and appreciation.

Chapter Twenty-one

AND THEN, ONE DAY, THEY CALLED ME from the church my mother had been halfheartedly attending. No church ever was the same as my father's church, but she attended loyally. The woman's voice, trying not to sound alarming, alarmed me.

"Mrs. Beaumont?" tentatively.

"Yes?" Hurry on, I thought.

Your mother's been at a meeting at the church. I'm calling from her home. She had a little spell. We brought her home. She's in bed. She seems to be all right now. I'll stay with her until you get here."

Alarm deepened into panic. Snatching at reassurance, I asked, "She's really all right now? Conscious? Did you call the doctor?"

"No. No," came the unknown voice. "We thought we should have you see her first. She seems to be fine now. Just blacked out, I guess. At church."

"Fine. I'll be right over." Action, not questioning, was needed now. Hugh was still at work, but would soon be home. I told the children, grabbed the car keys, and left for Mother's house. From here to there. Such a long way. Patience — impatience — frustration — calm — these feelings tumbled around all over my body and in my mind as I drove through tedious traffic on my way to face whatever lay ahead.

It had been coming on for some time, I knew, the high blood pressure so persistent, the little losses of memory, whole scenes, names, episodes. A tangle of thoughts and feelings lurched throughout my being.

I didn't want my mother to linger long in this life, helpless, a burden, as she so often feared. She had told me, "I don't want to be a burden. Promise me you'll put me in a nursing home if I get peculiar. I couldn't bear to be a burden. I saw my sister Katherine's mother-in-law almost kill her, so mean, so demanding. Sister Katherine waited on her hand and foot for years and one day in a better moment the old lady said to sister Katherine, she said, 'Katherine, when I get to heaven I'll save a place for you beside me,' and your Aunt Katherine said, 'Well, if I have to be beside that woman in heaven, I'd rather go to the other place!' I don't want you or anybody to have to care for me like that." And my mother would shake her head and laugh a bit and pick up her handwork again. But the message was clear, stayed with me, burrowed deep in the fiber of my understanding.

My mother didn't want to be a burden. And I understood, I thought. I didn't want her to be a burden either. I didn't want my deep love to erode with years of difficult care and torn loyalties between her needs and the needs of my husband and children. But I could not promise her. I couldn't bear the thought of her, confused, helpless, alone among strangers in her last years, this dear human being, unsung heroine of life, stronger in different ways than my father, earthier, more human, more real.

As I raced through the streets, pulling my awareness back to the task of driving the car, all of these thoughts and possibilities came to me in an intertwining jumble, all at once, in the strange way thoughts in stress often do. Fear and grief would almost overcome me, and then, the calm, rational voice within would say, "She's all right," the woman had said. "No cause to panic before you get there."

And then, I was there. And the kind, concerned lady from the church opened the door, showed relief that I had arrived and gestured to the bedroom. There lay my mother, tucked in bed, looking like a child, eyes searching my face, bewildered, anxious, but fully conscious. Relief and joy swept away all of those terrifying thoughts I'd driven with through the miles of city streets.

I knelt by the bed, reached for her hands and held them tight, I the mother, she the child. It seemed as though all of our life together was finding completion in this one overwhelming moment. I released my hand clasp, went into the living room to thank the lady and called the doctor, who said not to worry, to let her rest tonight and he would see her tomorrow. I returned to her room. I longed to be close to her, to touch as much of her as I possibly could. A surge of love, an instinct for which I offer eternal thanks, prompted me to get in bed beside her. I sat up, back against the bed frame, and stroked her forehead.

There were no words for long moments as I watched my mother intently. Her head was turned toward the wall where a small picture of my father, one of his last, hung in its silver frame. She was looking at it in silence, without moving. What was she thinking, feeling, remembering? What gave me the courage to ask the question that was in my mind and I felt must be in hers as well, the direct, honest question we are often too cautious, frightened, to ask? I'll never know. But if I never find a better word, Grace, again, is more than sufficient.

"Mama," I heard myself say, calmly and without fear, "when you" (and here I fell into that dread timidity, that awesome recoiling of using the word that intones finality) "when you — when your times comes" (why couldn't I just say the word die, but I couldn't, so I equivocated, softened, slid around) "when your time really comes and you — you're not here in the body anymore, do you think you will see Daddy again?"

I said "Daddy" plain and simple as though I were sixteen. I didn't say Father, your husband, Christian G. Hohn, but "Daddy" as we had both called him in the long ago land of my childhood.

Mother lay very still. The clock ticked. Gramma's clock. It was ticking away time for us now, as it would be for me in the many years ahead.

At last my mother broke the stillness. She turned her head away from the picture on the wall and looked at me. She gazed at me tenderly for a moment and slowly her brown eyes brightened and a mischievous twinkle brightened them again. I had asked her the Great Question concerning the After Life, the ultimate test of the Christian faith.

My mother, who had crocheted her way silently through endless discussions of the meaning of suffering, the possibility of Life After Death, twinkled at the question. Her look said to me that all those years of my father's suffer-ing and death, she had done her own thinking, kept her secret conclusion to herself, until now, when the reality of death and the possibility of immortality was before us both,

"Well," she said, still twinkling and reaching out from under the covers to pat my thin hand with her chubby one, "Well, Katya, I don't know. I don't really know about all that. But," and she smiled up at me to fully reassure me, "I do know that whatever it is, it's all right."

Whatever it is, it's all right. What could one small-souled daughter do, but tighten the clasp of her mother's hand, close her eyes and bow her head before such simple, yet powerful trust in Life, just as it is, birth and death, joy and sorrow.

A neighbor, who had been a nurse, offered to stay the night with my mother. I felt at peace as I drove slowly home to my husband and children.

Anna Marie Rockel
Hohn

The reflective mother,
here. A very honest, real
photo.

Anna in the 1924 Kiddie
Review in New Ulm,
Minnesota

The mama who loved to
dress up and perform! That
is her real hair, braided.

Chapter Twenty-two

MOTHER STAYED WITH US ON THE ISLAND a month in August 1959, and it was a perfect Mother-Daughter time, a gift from Life to Life as it has flowed through my mother to me, and now to my daughter.

I drove down to the airport in the Twin Cities to pick her up. The plane had been delayed, and then a dense fog all the way from the airport to the lake had delayed us further There were no cell phones in those days, no phone on the Island.

We arrived at the dock past midnight in the darkest of nights. Hunter, my patient, teenaged son had waited for more than two hours at our dock with our boat to take us across the lake to the Island.

Our boat was an eighteen-foot aluminum fishing boat with slippery seats and a ten-horse power motor. The summer nights in northern Minnesota are usually not so intense a black, but this was one. Hunter had only a feeble flashlight to guide us into the boat. My mother couldn't really see where to put her foot, so Hunter said, "Step here." And she stepped down from the dock three feet below her without a moment's hesitation. We steadied her a bit, but only as much as she seemed to need. Her trust was almost visible.

We arrived safely on the Island. She climbed out of the boat, and carrying her purse and bag of handwork, marched up to the Upper Lodge, stopping only once to take a deep breath. Kristy had thoughtfully lit the kerosene lamp in her room and turned down the covers. She hugged her beloved grandmother, and we each went to our own rooms to bed. I don't imagine my mother lay awake very long.

When she woke in the morning and gazed at the view, one- hundred feet down onto the blue lake through tall Norway pine, she shook her head in wonder as she breathed, "I never would have believed my daughter could own a place like this."

She delighted in everything, the old Upper Lodge, reminiscent of Camp Laf–a–Lot, only much bigger, the old pitchers, flat irons, coffee grinders, tin bread dough pan, the pump, the cast iron, wood-burning cook stove — all the things that still worked if you knew how to use them, which she did. All these things brought tears of affection and nostalgia to her eyes.

She pitched right in as though the time between then and now had disappeared.

Hugh and the children and I were finishing a painting job down at the Lower Lodge by the lake. Mother set herself the task of doing the cooking, preparing the main meal for readiness at noon as in the "olden days" at the lake and on the farm. When the noon-time meal was ready, she would walk down the path to fetch a pail of water from the pump and call us to dinner.

She was a sport, courageous, adventurous, full of energy and zest for life, in spite of the passage of years. She still had no fear of bats, (and there were clouds of them on the Island) nor storms and whitecaps on the lake, and she moved her seventy-six year old body up and down the path as though she were sixteen.

One day she watched us water ski and said, "I'd like to try that, too." So we pulled her through the water behind the boat at low throttle, on a home-made saucer. She laughed so hard she fell off.

There seemed to be an aura of wonder, relaxation and joy about her that summer that was sensed by all who met her, the neighbors across the lake who entertained her, and even the local dentist I took her to see, who called her a "cool cat" and commented on our relationship.

Totally gone was the cross and harried Mama of my teenage years and my father's long and excruciatingly painful illness. Her essence emerged as never before, trusting, energetic, full of good humor and love of life, her jolly laugh, the efficiency of movement that I see so wonderfully in my daughter now, her down-to-earth simplicity, were all fully there.

But the time on our beloved Balgillow Island had to end, of course, when we would pack up and leave our Eden for another year. Hugh had to fly back to California to work on the Beaver show, so that left me to drive the station wagon loaded with all we transported across the nation, including three children, our Black Labrador Retriever, Misky, and Mama, who was efficiently packed into a small suit case, make-up case, handwork and purse.

The trip was a long and tiring one. I drove too fast, as was the family custom.

One morning, already weary after driving across two barren Dakotas fighting a mean wind all the way, I asked our oldest son to drive. He had his learning permit, but was new to driving. Hugh had asked me not to let him drive, but I thought he was not only ready, but needed the sense of trust and responsibility that helping me drive would give him.

I felt at ease with Hunter at the wheel, my mother beside me, Kristy, Mark, our dog, our suitcases in the back. I was falling peacefully asleep when an earth-shaking crash woke me and changed my life forever.

Was I wrong? Wrong to go against my husband's wishes, wrong to lay that much responsibility on an already very serious young man? Were both Hugh and I wrong to set a pattern of too fast driving that my son naturally tried to emulate? What wrongness is there in the manufacture of faulty tires?

Now, in that moment of time, as I was hurtling through space, an all-at-once sensation of the interconnectedness, the essential oneness of all things on this earth, filled my being. In some wondrous, mystical sense I knew all through my mind, my body, my soul, that we are all wrong, often, and in many ways. With this instantaneous knowing in a nano-second of time, I felt the healing balm of forgiveness filling me, surrounding me — forgiveness of myself — of all others on this earth. With this All-is-One reality my whole being was filled with acceptance of Life, just as it is, just as my mother seemed to accept it.

Later, in reflecting on this experience, I was reminded of Carl Jung's response when he was asked, "Do you believe in God?" And he answered, "I do not believe. I know."

There is a knowing, beyond the reasoning of the mind. *All-is-One. All-is-forgiven.* This knowing is what I experienced while flying through the air that fateful day.

Numbers of cars stopped and offered help. They had seen it all, seen the car hurtle through the air, saw my mother ejected from our vehicle and tossed as high as the telephone wires by the impact. They saw me tumbling across a ditch, through a barbed-wire fence (over, under — who knows) and without a second's stop, landing on my feet and rushing to our crumpled station wagon.

There my three children sat, stunned into silence, shocked, but safe. Hunter sat benumbed with the driver's wheel still in his hands, broken from its shaft. Kristy and Mark and our Black Labrador, ears flattened, leg twitching, lay in the back seat amidst the jumbled suit cases and sleeping bags. They were safe! No tears, no screams, no hysteria from my brave, beloved children. But where, oh where in God's earth was my mother?

The children knew enough to leave the car as soon as they could, should it burst into flames. Stunned as they were, they searched for mother with me. We groped our way through the tall prairie grass, searching for her.

There she lay, ten — twenty feet from the car, down on her side, still as death, nestled in the grasses as though she had fallen into a profound sleep.

One of the men who stopped, owned a garage. He examined our station wagon and determined there had undoubtedly been two blow outs at the same time on the same side of the station wagon. No one could have controlled the car in that situation. He had called an ambulance and the police on his car phone. There was nothing more we could do now, but wait.

How could I put my feelings into words? They were there in my body, my mind, in all of my being, pulling apart, leaving emptiness filled only by the strange wrenching we call anguish. I felt pulled toward my mother with unbearable longing. If only I could take her up in my arms and rise up together out of here, out of this place of too terrifying reality. I touched her with cold fingers. She was still warm, but I could not see her chest rise in breathing.

Taut with fear, I stared down brash time, lived out the arrival of the sheriff, the ambulance, the checking and rechecking of the children, the trip to the hospital, the doctor's report. Children shocked. Mercifully had no injuries. Boys all right. Kristy vomiting, needing a night's stay in the hospital.

But Mother — broken hip, collapsed kidney, very seriously injured.

"We'll care for her here," the doctor said, "but when she comes out of the coma, she'll have to be flown to Cheyenne to have her hip pinned, the injured kidney removed, perhaps. With her history of high blood pressure, that's dangerous. We'll have to see."

How can such intensity be lived through as though in a mist, and at the same time every detail sharply defined, the impress of each moment engraved for all time in every cell, tissue, synapse, and in the marrow of my bones.

Remembering the kindness of the people of Gillette, Wyoming, I am still warmed. They brought us clothes, food and reassurance. The doctor took us spotting antelope that evening after visiting hours at the hospital. He brought us fresh spring water and found us a motel. All of this still warms me.

I tucked my dearly loved children into their beds in the motel, left them alone and went back to the hospital.

Mother had regained consciousness, but lay very still. I was riveted to her bedside, part of me also with my children who needed me, too. They had each other, but was that enough?

After a time — how long, I do not know, Mother's eyes opened. She saw me and tried a smile. She whispered faintly, "You all right?"

"Yes, Mother, I am."

"And the children?"

"Yes, Mama, they're all right, too."

She closed her eyes then, a small sigh expressing her relief. After a moment, she quietly and simply said, "It's best this way," and seemed to fall asleep.

Did she sense my presence? She must have known I was there with her, waiting. I held her hand. She acknowledged the gesture with a feeble smile.

With her eyes still closed, she whispered, "Have you eaten?"

That is when the brimming cup spilled over. Here lay my earthly mother, mortally wounded, but in total identity with the Great Mother, the essence of nurturing.

"Go, take care of the children," were her last words before she fell asleep with the drug the doctor had given her.

I had called Hugh and he arrived the next day, dumbfounded when he saw the demolished station wagon and realized the miracle of our survival. All the arrangements were made by him and the doctor to fly my mother immediately to Cheyenne, the nearest city of any size. Hugh drove a rented car with the children, our dog, and me. We sped across the miles, but arrived several hours after the plane with my mother and a special nurse.

Mama was in a deep sleep when I finally saw her in her room in the hospital. I thought she might have slipped into a coma again. Her lustrous hair had been loosened and she lay motionless in the bed. I enclosed her limp hand in both my own.

Suddenly, she sat straight up in bed, hair streaming down her back, eyes opened wide, gazing with wonder straight ahead.

"Let's go!" she said, with a strange and potent energy. Then, she fell back, closed her eyes and said no more.

The specialist at the hospital had examined her, verified the broken hip and the seriousness of her condition. He timidly said that after the hip had been pinned, she could, perhaps, be flown to Denver and put on an artificial kidney. He was not at all reassuring that she would survive the trip. He left us saying we would see how she was doing in the morning.

I knew, with the sureness of uncomplicated love that my mother would not want just to survive. Her oft-repeated plea, "Promise me, you'll not let me be a burden," sounded in both ear and heart; and even though I could never promise her anything, I knew beyond a shadow of a doubt, she would not want extraordinary measures used to help her just to survive. There was no conflict within me, and before this moment, conflict could have been my middle name.

Hugh comforted me as best he could. We found a motel, tried to enjoy a fine dinner with the children and went numbly to bed.

About four o'clock in the morning a vivid and terrifying dream awakened me. I saw my mother's head — a death's head — in a frighteningly clear image. In the dream, a nurse came to me through the transparent outline of my mother's face and said, "Your mother is dying."

I wakened, sobbing loudly, beyond comfort, and shared my dream with Hugh.

"It's only a dream," my husband said, gently. "You're exhausted. Why don't you take a warm bath and dress and we'll go to the hospital, even though its four in the morning."

I knew he was wise. I drew the bath water, and just as I was about to sink in, the telephone rang.

It was the hospital. The doctor himself.

"I'm sorry to tell you this, but your mother has just passed away."

"Let's go, Mother. Let's go! If I could, I would take you there, wherever, whatever there may be — that place which you have said, in your infinite trust is 'all right'. I would pick you up in my arms as you did me when I was a child, and carry you there, enfolded in everlasting loving arms."

But life and death are not structured that way. You must go on to whatever it is, and I must stay here to fulfill the life given to me, through you, with all its joy and sorrows, imperfections, privileges and responsibilities, such as my own children, whose confidence in life must be severely shaken. They need me now.

So my need and longing for you must find a place, without guilt, in the deep recesses of my being, beside the place of honor in which I place you.

For I do love and honor you, my mother. We have had a wonderful mother-daughter life together. There have been stormy times, tender times, wondrous times. I do not look at all like you. I take after my father and the Hohn family. I am, still, a father's daughter. I was tall and slender and fair. You were and are short (didn't Hugh call you 'Shorty'?) and chubby as well, with that incredible dark, thick hair. I am intellectual, introverted, passive. You are immediate, sensual, active. I'll never cook like you, do handwork like you, move about the house and yard with such vigorous efficiency.

And yet, you are in me, all around and through me. With each year that passes, I see more of you in the face I see in the mirror. I'm wrinkling and puckering in the same places around the mouth, the eyes. I have lost height and gained weight, becoming less and less the tall, "moonlight blonde" of my brief film career days.

My hands are shortening with veins and dark spots showing in the same places as in yours. When I am happy and excited, I find myself cozying myself as you used to do, arms crossed in front of me, hugging myself tightly as if only in that way could I contain the joy.

But deeper than all of that, your sense of immediacy, your trust and love of life, all of it, just as it is, has slowly replaced the anxious striving for perfection that was so much a part of the Great Father within me.

I find myself wanting to nurture and reverence all of life now, my imperfect self, every leaf, flower, bird and child; and to be fully there in every moment, in everyday things like washing a dish, writing a letter, taking a bath, watching the sun set and the stars come out. This kind of knowledge and experience of reality you have instilled in me, not through words, creeds, dictum, aspirations, but through the life you lived in the here and now.

My gratitude is boundless. Thank you, my mother.

The process of grieving for my mother was a long one. It does not seem to be altogether ended, after all these long years. I wonder if there is not in all of us from time to time, in moments of discouragement, pain, and loss of hope, a deep longing for a haven, a resting place, a home, that we associate with the Great Mother — a yearning to return to the womb, the Source from which we all came, the Great Return to Paradise, to God, whoever, whatever He/She may be. Or perhaps it is a longing to pass beyond ourselves as we now are, to keep changing and growing no matter how old we become, just as we continually developed within the womb, until we were ready to emerge as a new, fresh being into the experience of Life on Earth.

Such thoughts and feelings were part of my grieving, and in the midst of the process, I became aware that only that one time when I asked, "Do you believe when you — when you leave this life that you will see Daddy?" Only that once did I ever have a philosophical or religious discussion with my Mama. Strange, I never thought of her as particularly religious or spiritual. She never yielded in moments of perplexity to theological platitudes such as "It's God's will" or "Just have faith." None of that.

She laughed heartily when she was happy, cried when she was sad, spanked the dish water when she was angry. She cleaned, cooked, did endless handwork, entertained guests, served her minister's wifely duties teaching Sunday School, being president of the Missionary Society, though she didn't really enjoy it, singing in the choir — alto. She fought battles with tyrants my father was too yielding to fight, she fussed, complained, pursed her lips in disapproval. But she never once, to my knowledge, questioned her destiny, strived for perfection, or railed against life. She simply lived it and accepted it.

After the funeral service which took place in Nebraska in the church my father grew up in, after placing her body to rest beside my father in the country church yard and returning to California, settling my children in school and my husband to work, it was time, once again, for the "sweeping of the heart."

It was time to open the door of my mother's neat little house, let the impact of her familiar things sweep over me and start to sort through her belongings to settle her very small estate.

It was then my final realization of the essence of my mother really came to me. Tucked in among all the neatly filed letters, bills, receipts, calendars, recipes, daily reminders, in her desk and in her kitchen and bedroom drawers, I found little pieces of paper written in her still clear, beautiful Spencerian penmanship.

There on these fragments were words to hymns and Bible verses that must have meant much to her and that I had no idea she even thought about. It seemed so uncharacteristic of her. I only remember her singing, in her rich, alto voice, the hymn, "Work, for the night is coming." That is all I thought she remembered.

But I was so wrong, I now knew. There had been so much loneliness in those last years, and I saw evidence of her struggle to deal with it, very much in her own way. She addressed herself to the task of passing beyond herself as she was, and in her aging years, becoming an even greater person than she had been.

She must have instinctively known that in taking pen in hand and pressing the meaningful words down onto paper, she was impressing in and from her body, solace for her soul.

"The Lord is my shepherd." All of the twenty-third psalm.

"Oh Love that will not let me go . . ." All of that hymn poem.

And most beautifully and carefully of all, all of the thirteenth chapter of First Corinthians, down to, "I give to you these three things, Faith, Hope, and Love, and the greatest of these is Love."

This was the essence of my mother, and it came to me then that her life's story was a re-enactment of the ancient myth of Demeter, the goddess whose beloved only daughter was stolen from her and taken away to the Underworld. Demeter's grief was long and deep. But in her sorrowing she grew to greatness, emerged from her long stay in her own barren ground of being, and took her place among the most revered of holy ones. Her daughter was returned to her for part of each year, and life flourished for all. In the days to come, will I recognize Persephone, Demeter's daughter, in me?

In the living of our own lives, we unconsciously relive stories that are truly immortal. They are patterns repeated untold times throughout human history. Something in each of us lives on — and on.

Thank you, my mother. Thank you, Life.

In this moment now, as I finish these memoirs of my mother, and yearly become more "the mother of me," I want to share a dream I had several months after her death:

> *I am walking up the hill on the Island toward the old lodge. On my back I am carrying a gunny sack filled with manure. The manure is my mother's body, transforming into rich compost even as I walk. The material is inert, but seems to be alive in some mysterious way.*
>
> *When I reach the top of the hill, I place the manure-compost in a wooden container like the old wooden bucket of my grandmother's. When I finish filling the container, I plant African violets in it.*
>
> *Time passes, as it does in dreams, and as I stand and watch the container, green stems appear, leaves emerge, unfold, and purple flowers appear. Each flower has a golden center. They are hardy. And beautiful beyond imagining. They glow with life. I touch the soil around the flowers and thank the earth that holds them. I feel blessed.*

〜 *Chapter Twenty-three* 〜

FOR MY FATHER. It has been a long time, seventy years, I believe, since we have talked to one another. And I long to do so now. The only way I can reach you is in Active Imagination, a pathway to the Unconscious, other than dreams, which Carl Jung described and proposed. I now close my eyes, relax, and let an image of you, as I remember you, come into my mind.

You smile, but do not speak. It is I who must begin the conversation.

I have just finished my memoirs, *Becoming the Mother of Me*, which came to closure with the death of my mother, your wife, Anna Marie Rockel Hohn.

So much has happened since her death. Wanting to write of my past, I had pulled the camera of my mind back for the long shot, to see and experience the vivid scenes and dreams of my long ago life. It has been a wondrous journey, both painful and joyous. Anna Marie died in 1959, almost fifty years ago (did you have a way of knowing this?) and the many changes in my life since then and now are very great.

Hugh Beaumont's and my children matured, married, and moved on into independent and fulfilled lives of their own. Our empty nest brought us to the realization that we needed to bring to closure the legal aspects of our relationship and move on ourselves into independent ways. We had been more father-daughter than husband and wife.

Leaving the Upper Midwest, and my particular background for Hollywood — alone — still a mere adolescent, was too great a leap for me. I needed a father. Someone who knew something of life. Someone who would not stand in front of me, shielding me from the world and making my decisions for me; but stand behind me, and whose strength I could feel in the bones of my back. Hugh had been well prepared for this role by his own family history, and I gratefully accepted all of his fatherly guidance. If he was the father, then I surely must have remained his child.

It seems ironic now that the most successful role in his film career was as the father in *Leave it To Beaver*. Fatherhood, both on screen and off, was thrust upon him and I am deeply sorry that I did not understand the heaviness of this lifelong burden for him. I never once said "thank you" to him for all that he did. I took it all for granted. In a letter, Barbara Billingsley (June in *Leave It to Beaver*) expressed a wish that I have often felt — that Hugh could have lived to to experience the impact that the show had on so many lives. He contributed so much to its success. He wrote a few episodes, directed a few; but most importantly, he set the tone for the wisdom and concern of the father. I understand now that as fine and many-sided an actor Hugh was, he would have loved a greater variety of roles as the years passed. Gratefully, Hugh and I stayed in touch and remained friends.

I am now married to a most remarkable man, Fred Doty, with whom you would have had much in common. My brother Roland enthusiastically married us in a simple ceremony. Rolly and Fred had many wonderful conversations together and I imagine you and Fred also might have shared ideas and experiences in both of your most meaningful ministries.

Fred and I worked together as therapists until our retirement, traveled happily for a number of years, and finally settled down, back in my Minnesota, where we both are traveling through the vicissitudes of aging, with its own joys and challenges. Together we have seven children, eleven grandchildren and seven great-grandchildren.

In this moment now, I remember one of the last conversations we had the summer of your body's death. It took place behind the shed at Camp-Laf-a-Lot, where we had bonfires many summer evenings. You were in a reflective mood, contemplating your end of life's journey. I remember, now, the sadness in your face as you spoke to me.

> *I do not know, beyond a shadow of a doubt, my daughter, what will happen to me in the After-Life, or even, whether or not there is one. That is part of Life's Mystery, before which I bow in reverent awe. But this I know, in this known life, you have been a delight to me, and I am deeply saddened that I have to let you go. I would like to live on to see what happens to you. Beyond that, if there is any way, any way at all, that I can reach you beyond the veil, I will do so.*
>
> *Part of my being looks forward to the end of this body-life of pain, and beginning the mysterious journey ahead. So, if I may, I say good-bye to you now, while I am conscious, and in Shakespeare's words "love you well which I must leave 'ere long."*

I was so young then, with the longest stretch of my years ahead of me, that I took your sharing for granted. Now, in aging, as I face the brevity of life before me, I can much more fully understand your sadness at having to leave "Unfinished Business" behind you.

But in this moment now, in active imagination, I can and will continue the death-interrupted conversation: I do not know, my father, whether or not you tried, and failed, to get through to me after your death. I was so filled with the rational, the thinking head trip, of not seeming or being too emotional, too "feminine", that I may have missed messages that were there.

(In my imagination, I see you smile now, a familiar twinkle in your eyes.)

It was only several years ago that I sat in our living room in Mankato, Minnesota, with Fred, looking out and down into our beautiful ravine. I had finished my first novel, *A Long Year of Silence* and was feeling discouraged about its ever being published. I was remembering your calling the whip-poor-wills in the ravine in the country around New Ulm. Without any conscious connection to anything that I was aware of, I turned to Fred and asked, "Fred, we all know Kahlil Gibran's book, *The Prophet,* but did you know that he also wrote a book called *Jesus, the Son of Man*?"

"Yes," Fred answered quickly. "I have it in my library." And he immediately went to look for it, found it, and together we looked though it with appreciation.

Less than a week later, I received a small package in the mail, wrapped in brown paper, opened it, and there was the book, *Jesus, the Son of Man*, by Kahlil Gibran! With the book was a letter from a much appreciated friend of my adolescent years, "My wife and I were going through our library and thought you should have this."

Inside the fly leaf, Father, was your signature, "Christian G. Hohn, 1929."

Awe and wonder silenced both Fred and me. I had told him of your being so much ahead of your time, and of how much you two would have appreciated and enjoyed each other. Now, the evidence was before us. Together we checked through the table of contents to remind us of some of the essays in the book. Some of them were critical of Jesus, giving the reader a broad glimpse into the way Jesus was perceived by his detractors in his own time.

A number of the essays were checked, giving me a glimpse into your inner struggles that became clear to me for the first time in my life. Anger and sexuality were those with faint check marks behind them. Was this a message you were trying to convey to me — that my adored father was a *human* human being?

For the first time in my life, also, I took this incident as a synchronistic event

— a meaningful coincidence, not pushed from behind by cause and effect, but pulled forward by the urge toward consciousness and meaning. It was a hallowed realization, not unlike flying through the air after the accident in Wyoming and experiencing, powerfully, *All-is-One*, and *All-is-forgiven*.

(You still do not speak my Father, in this active imagination, but tears fill your eyes.)

After receiving this message, and taking it seriously, I renewed my search for a publisher, looked for a Minnesotan on the internet and found one, Daniel Hoisington of Edinborough Press. He advertised as being interested in history and social issues. My grandson, Jesse Beaumont, had just graduated from the University of Edinburgh in Scotland, so, in a quixotic mood, I sent the manuscript to Hoisington. He liked it, agreed to meet me in New Ulm, and during that visit offered me a contract. I was speechless. I remained benumbed when I learned, for the first time, that Hoisington had been hired by the city of New Ulm, Minnesota, to research and write its history!

Writing the story of New Ulm, and having it published, was a turning for me. I never heard you talk about that time during World War I, the degree of German-American prejudice, your heart-break as you endured it. Was it too painful to talk about? It was my mother whose hearty, honest indignation gave me a glimpse of what that painful time must have been like for you and the citizens of New Ulm.

Now, in this late-life emergence as a published writer, I have looked back at my early years with wonder and appreciation. My brief film career has emerged as being of great interest to many folks, and even though it was but a minor part of my life, I have accepted the fact that it was, and is, intriguing to many, so far from the Hollywood scene. I was more of a very small shooting star, blazing briefly across the heavens, and I only regret that I didn't appreciate the opportunity opened to me, the kindness of so many people, the exposure to a broader range of personalities and experiences, softening my judgments and opening my mind and heart.

In looking back, and seeing you now with imagination's vision, I can believe, if you had lived, you very well may have gone with me to Hollywood, and met some of the people who were so generous, interesting — and, yes, kind! I can imagine you and Gregory La Cava might have become fast friends, he having never met anyone quite like you. But that was not the way it was meant to be, and the image of your going to Hollywood with me does not take one bit away from the depth and wonder of all you taught me that became a genuine part of my being.

It was from you I learned to experience myself as part of the natural world. As a tall two-legged, you bent down with me to watch a colony of ants, tirelessly working together, carrying tiny grains of sand to their hills to build their homes. Sunrise, sunset, shape changing moon, faithful day journeying of the sun, the emergence of stars patterns in the night sky — you shared all these with me from my earliest days. You did not seem to be or feel apart from all of these great natural happenings. You were not the superior observer, but a part of the infinite whole. You did not teach me this attitude with words, but with your quiet presence beside me, sharing the experiences with wonder and appreciation.

It was you who introduced me to the world of literature, great books, poetry especially, which touched a part of my being larger, deeper, other, than just my mind. I still hear you reciting such poems, some of them in German — "*Du bist wie eine Blume* — You are like a flower," or Emerson, "Beauty through my senses stole, I yielded myself to the perfect whole." Some of these stanzas still echo in my mind, and I feel sure, ultimately influenced my desire to write, to BE a writer, to translate into the music of words what cannot be expressed or understood so well any other way.

And there was music itself, the love for it shared by my mother. As a small child, you woke me just before midnight one Christmas Eve, carried me in your arms into our living room to hear, through our squawky radio, all the way from Germany, the great contralto Madame Schumann-Heinck sing "*Stille Nacht*". And your own rich baritone voice dramatically singing Schubert's "*Der Erlkönig, the Erlking*", in German, gave me shivers.

These experiences are unforgettable. But there was so much more that came to me through you. There was the call to be "on the growing edge," to internalize the positive message of compassion, lived out in the lives of Jesus of Nazareth and of the Buddha. In this sense my education will never be finished as long as I live, and is deeper than my child-like striving for personal perfection and the judgmental attitudes that go with it.

I feel sure it was not your intent to burden me with the dictum, "Be ye perfect even as our Father in Heaven is perfect." As a child, I translated the things you said literally, according to the standards of the time. This meant, then, not being angry, sexual, jealous, rude; but being modest, unassuming, frugal, forgoing the need to be the "one and only". Times have changed, and what was considered perfect then, is psychologically unsound and certainly not popular today. I know in my heart you had no intention whatsoever to "lay a guilt trip on me" ; but rather, as the way you then could express your love and hope for a fulfilled and meaningful life for me. In adulthood, it is my task to see this difference. My way to come to this awareness and integration of my shadow, and my unlived life as well, was to really see and experience, the feet-on-the ground wisdom and strength of the Feminine, as exemplified in my own earthy mother. This does not denigrate all that you taught me, all of you that is still in me, but to put all of that in perspective and become more "the mother of me" — to accept my humanity, my ordinariness.

I have been, and am, singularly blessed with wonderful parents, my father, my mother — both of you. It is never to late to say, "Thank you!"

In writing these words, I am reminded of a sermon brother Rolly preached in Crookston, the time he filled in for you when you were in the hospital in Minneapolis. One Sunday morning he asked the congregation to think about what they considered to be the greatest sin, and the following Sunday, he would share his vote. The sanctuary was filled to the brim that Sunday morning. His choice for the greatest sin? *Ingratitude!* That thought and all that it implies has stayed with me all through my lengthening life.

I have learned a great deal in these eighty-six years, and there is still the vast Unknown before me. Facing this reality, I am reminded of my favorite sermon of yours, "Stewards of Mystery", and I feel both comfort and awe in the words of C. G. Jung with which I bring my conversation with you to closure, and let you go:

"Life is not so much a puzzle to be solved, as a Mystery to be lived."

In imagination again, I see you smile, and without a word, rise up and walk toward me. You hold out your arms, enclosing me securely and warmly. You release me now, turn and slowly walk away, fading quietly into the distance.

⤜⟶ Days of Now ⟵⤛

"To regret one's own experience, is to arrest one's own development. To
deny one's own experience is to put a lie in the lips of one's own life. It is
no less than a denial of the soul." — *Oscar Wilde*

It is no longer Then. It is Now.
I have rewound the film in he camera of my mind
locked illuminated memories in compact discs.
Late life tasks of aging lie before me.

Time to lay down the burdens of regret,
the tiny accolades of fame,
retrace my valley of the shadow-way
struggling up mountains
slip-sliding back
traveling flat barren lands between,
making soul.
Time to accept imperfections, incompletions
bound to persist.

I want to be there when I die,
push my way out of the womb of this life into the vast unknown.
Before I slowly go to meet my death
I say "thank you" to all whose lives intertwined with mine
teaching me truths I could not learn alone.
"Thank you," body, for all you do for the me I am just beginning to know,
ceaselessly beating heart, its rhythms slow and stumbling,
crumbling bones, womb no longer there.
Three times it cradled life
filling me with bundles of infinite possibilities.
"Thank you," eyes and ears, that brought the outer world to me, dimming now
as memory slowly fades.

I cannot conceive of Nothingness — Eternity — Infinity —
concepts my small mind cannot grasp.
So now I say, as my honored mother said,
"I do not know about the After Life, but whatever it is, it is all,
all right."